Alone with Abe

Dan Adams

Ten|16
PRESS

www.ten16press.com - Waukesha, WI

For information, please contact:

Ten | 16
PRESS

www.ten16press.com
Waukesha, WI

Cover art by Jayden Ellsworth
Art Director: Kaeley Dunteman

To my parents, whom I owe my greatest gratitude in the pursuit of my writing career. Thank you for always understanding the voices in my head.

Alone with Abe

Dan Adams

CAST OF CHARACTERS

(accents in parentheses)

Abe (Scottish)
Dan Adams (Midwest American)
Damon (German)
Dick Goldschmidt (Old English)
Emma Kenda (Texan American)
Charles
Lewis Strange (Midwest American)
Michele Strange (Texan American)
Ox (Midwest American)
Rita Flemming (French)
Seth (British)
Tank (Midwest American)

Chuck: This is the story of the game. It is played every day. There are winners. There are losers. For one man to create so many of both is reason for that person to become insane. I am the world of the insane and this is my story.

Dan Adams: My name is Lewis Strange . . .

SCENE 1

Setting:

The room is dark with a faint light. In that light, Lewis Strange is sitting at a table with two chairs located in the middle of the room. Lewis is facing the darkest side of the room, opposite the window. The window behind him on which the shade has been drawn eliminates any outside light. The back wall of the room has a mirror, and despite the darkness, the audience can make out the reflection of Lewis's side.

The floor of the room is black. The walls appear to have been white a long time ago but are now stained with a grayish color.

The table that Lewis is sitting near is similar to a table that one would find in any American high school cafeteria. On top of the table are a notebook, a pen, and two cups of coffee that are still evaporating steam into the air.

Abe is standing behind Lewis. His head is only inches from Lewis as he pushes at him, attempting to bring him back to reality.

Damon is standing silently near the mirror. His only goal is to observe the entire situation that is occurring in front of him. However, an expression of agitation is noticeably upon his face. He appears to frown more with each passing move or statement made by Abe.

7

Rita is seated at a chair that rests against the wall opposite the mirror. She is on the edge of her seat holding a look of anticipation. However, the audience is also able to notice that she appears very nervous and shaky as she smokes her cigarette.

Michele Strange stands beside Rita. She is dressed in a skirt and a blouse. A gun is noticeably lodged in a gun holder that hangs over her right shoulder. Her face is filled with anticipation and excitement. She appears to be on the verge of gaining something that she has been waiting on for a long time.

Lewis: Shut up!

Abe: Dammit! Everyone out!

Michele: But Abe, we almost had him . . .

Abe: We didn't almost have anything! We've never come any closer to reality with him than we've come to the imaginary ourselves!

Rita: Professionally, he's right. Your brother may never come back to reality. We have done all we can for him. As the old saying goes, the ball is in hands now.

Michele: No . . . It just can't be true. There has to be some way to help him. He's lost so much throughout the years.

Abe: I'm afraid these are the cold facts Michele, but I still remain confident that we will pull your brother out of it. We will bring him back to reality, but when exactly that will happen . . . I can't really say, I mean . . . I thought he would be healed by now.

Damon: He's nuts, Abe! He always has been nuts, and he will always be nuts!

Abe: Shut up! . . . Dammit! . . . By saying that, you could have set him back five years! Get out! Everyone out! I don't want you harming him any more than you already have! . . . I said, clear the room! Now!

Rita: But Abe . . .

Abe: I don't want you to damage my work anymore.

Rita: Don't you mean *our* work?

Abe: Of course . . . You know I do. I'm sorry. I was just angry. It's just that Lewis's mind is so fragile. He could be lost forever if these outbursts continue to happen.

Rita: He's right. Everyone, clear out. We'll switch rooms and regroup.

Abe: Thank you.

Rita: I mean you, too, Abe!

Abe: I know, I know . . . Damon, I want to see you outside. Stay by the door and don't disappear. I have something important to talk to you about.

Damon: Sure.

Michele: Is that all you're going to do? Without him sane, I have no family. My parents will never go to jail, and I will never prove their guilt.

Abe: There are more important things than your revenge on your parents.

Michele: Like what?

Abe: One thing is the health of your brother! His case is very rare, but solving it could help many people. Those that are sane like you, Rita, and myself. Or those that are insane and suffering from similar cases to Lewis's.

Rita: He's right. If you continue to work with us, Lewis will eventually regain his sanity. When that happens, we as doctors will solve a number of cases that have been mysteries for years in the psychological field of study. You, also, will solve a case. You will be able to put your past behind you and move on with a bright police career. And don't forget Lewis. He will gain a world that has been lost to him for most of his life: reality.

Michele, Rita, and Damon clear the room, leaving Abe alone with Lewis. Throughout the entire dispute and conversation between Abe, his colleagues, and Michele, Lewis has been speaking to the voices in his head, as he has for years. The lights dim, while a single spotlight is aimed directly at Abe.

Abe: Lewis . . . Why? Why can't I bring you back? Back to the world you once loved. Why can't you let your sister go? . . . Her death wasn't your fault. It was an accident. Was life so cruel? Were your parents so awful that you forever became insane? . . . Were they so cruel that they permanently chased you away forever? Were you so alone that you had to make a world of imaginary friends from your enemies in the real world? . . . Oh, Lewis, your world has become a world of dreams and a world of the insane . . . If only you had a friend, someone that I could talk to . . . Someone that you could talk to . . . Someone who could penetrate that wall between reality and the imaginary. If only there were another case as serious as yours. Then I would know . . . I would know what to do to make you healthy . . . whole . . . a man again, instead . . . instead of this whimpering child that you pretend to be.

The spotlight is turned off, and the curtain is closed.

SCENE 2

Setting:

Damon and Abe are located in a hallway just outside Lewis's room. Michele and Rita can be seen walking away from the audience. They enter a room on the left side of the hallway and quickly fall out of the vision of the audience.

The hallway is very busy. Due to the bright lights, many people can be seen moving briskly from room to room. The men are all dressed in white pants and jackets. Meanwhile, the women are all wearing white dresses.

The lights in the hallway are fluorescent. They are attached to the ceiling of the hallway, about nine feet in the air.

Amidst this very active and bright hallway, Abe and Damon are standing in an area that is virtually isolated. People seem to avoid coming anywhere near where they stand. Lewis's room is next to them and they are at the front of the stage, giving the audience the impression that Lewis's room is in the front left corner of the stage.

There are virtually no chairs or decorations in this part of the hallway. It is very isolated, and the blandness seems to give the impression that no one cares about this room or this patient.

The audience is able to see Lewis sitting in a dark area on the left side of the stage. He is talking to himself in a dark room, oblivious to the conversation that Abe and Damon are having in the hallway.

In the hallway, Abe looks through a small square plate of glass at Lewis while he speaks to Damon. Abe is noticeably angry. His face is red, and his hair is frantically running in a thousand different directions.

Meanwhile, Damon is standing with his back to Lewis and the room. He appears very arrogant and cocky. It also is noticeable that Damon glances at his watch numerous times throughout the scene, implying that he feels impatient with Abe. The audience is meant to get the impression that Damon feels as though he is being detained.

Damon: You wanted to speak to me.

Abe: Yes! If I ever hear you call a patient of mine or any other doctor nuts, I will personally rip your tongue off and throw your ass out on the street!

Damon: But, Doctor, I . . .

Abe: But nothing! Just because you have suddenly become published in the field concerning the mentally insane, you still work for me. As long as you work for me and you are below me, you will do things the way I say they are to be done. Is that clear?

Damon: Yes, I . . .

Abe: You nothing! I can't tolerate your disrespect for those that are sick . . . the insane have rights, and I will be damned if I am going to allow you to call a man nuts to his face in front of his family and, more importantly, in front of my colleagues . . .

Damon: Maybe I should leave then? Or work with another patient? Wouldn't that be a suitable response or solution to this entire dispute between us?

Abe: I would love to see you leave. But I can't, because I feel . . . No, I know that in some way you can make Lewis sane again. He seems attached to you for some reason, and I don't want to ruin his chance for recovery because of some silly disagreement we are having.

Damon: So I stay, and I say what I feel because you need me.

Abe: No! You stay and keep your mouth shut. If you have an opinion, you wait and talk to me about it after the session . . . Are we clear?

Damon: Can I speak freely with you now?

Abe: Yes, but keep your tone down. There are many people that wander these hospital halls with their ears glued to the walls. That's a lesson you will learn when you get out on your own.

Damon: No one in this hallway cares whether or not Lewis becomes sane. As a matter of fact, no one who was in that room just now cares if he becomes sane. Everyone has their own reason and their own motive for seeing this through.

Abe: I'm not sure if I see your point. Are you saying you care? Because if you are, I have to disagree. I mean, after all, you called a patient nuts.

Damon: That's exactly my point!

Abe: I'm not sure I understand?

Damon: I called Lewis nuts to see if anyone would take offense to my comment, but everyone in that room only confirmed what I'm telling you.

Abe: How can you say that? I . . .

Damon: Don't start, Doctor. Don't get angry with me because deep down, you know I'm right. My comment was rude and offensive, yet Rita never even flinched. Michele, his own sister, didn't even flick an eyelid. There is no way for Lewis to take offense, since he can't hear me or understand what I'm saying.

Abe: There is one way Lewis could hear what you said . . .

Damon: I know. If he thinks I'm speaking to him as a doctor, he might have been able to hear what I said. But do you for one moment really believe that Lewis could think I was his doctor?

Abe: I do.

Damon: Well . . . then . . . maybe it will do him some good to be called a nut. Maybe it will make him see what he is seen as in reality.

Abe: That's where you are wrong. You are too young to remember the true history of patients like Lewis. Every time someone does what you did in there, our chances of healing him decrease. He drifts further away from reality and further into the imaginary.

Damon: That may be true, but the fact remains that you can't help him the way you would help another patient. Logic then follows that you may not be able to hurt him the same ways you hurt other patients.

Abe: You are saying . . .

Damon: I'm saying that he is different. He's trapped because he wants to be trapped. You know that as well as I do. Or at least, I would hope you do.

Abe: I do.

Damon: So do Rita and Michele. The only way you can bring Lewis back is to make him want to come back. Reality no longer has anything to offer that he can't find in the imaginary. But the imaginary has Sara, his sister, the one who died and can never come back to reality.

Abe: Once again, you are wrong. No one wants to be mentally disturbed. No one wants to be insane. He wants help. He wants to be free. Now, all I have to do is find the key . . . the key that will unlock his mind from the insanity.

Damon: Doctor, there isn't a key for everything. Look at the door. It is hooked up to an identification card. You need a code, a card, and a fingerprint that matches the one on the automatic scanner.

Abe: There is a key, and I will find it. I will discover the way to unlock or decode his mind. I will save him. He is my patient. I am his only friend. I will always be there for him, and if you continue to damage my work, my years of research, studying, and therapy with careless, carefree comments that make you feel good, I will destroy you by destroying your career. I will make sure you never work anywhere again! And don't think my reputation isn't strong enough to do it, because it is.

Damon: If you are as good as you say you are, you should be able to handle a few bumps.

Abe: It's not only the damage to my work and my years of investment that I am worried about. It's the damage to his sister that scares me. She is at an emotional stability point right now, and I don't want to see her break.

Damon: That's what I'm trying to say. You don't have to worry about that because his sister doesn't care. All she wants is her freedom, and she will use anyone or anything to get it. Lewis is the key to that freedom. He is the key to throwing her parents in jail for the rest of their lives. The only way she can do that is to free Lewis. He is a pawn in the way of her freedom.

Abe: I think you're wrong again. You think you know a lot, but I know you're wrong because she loves him. She needs family that will care because her freedom, as you put it, will mean nothing if she doesn't have someone to share it with.

Damon: Do you really believe that?

Abe: I do.

Damon: That's too bad, because then she has fooled you more than Lewis has. I think you need to review her story again. Ask her about her past. Ask her for the truth, because you will find a surprise.

Abe: You've got my attention. What kind of surprise will I find?

Damon: The kind that will free Lewis. The kind that will clear up his past and give you the key that you are searching for.

Abe: If you know something, Damon, and you're not telling me . . .

Damon: Abe, I have already told you what you need to know. You just refuse to listen. If you really want to save Lewis, speak to Michele. Don't hear the words, but really listen to what she says. Listen to the pain, anger, disgust, and sadness in her voice. Then listen to Lewis speak. The similarities will tell you more than you need to know.

Abe: What do you know?

Damon: I know that I was wrong to do what I did in that room, but it was the only way I could get your attention. It was the only way I could alert you to the truth.

Abe: What truth?

Damon: The truth of the past: Michele's past, Lewis's past, Rita's past, my past, and your past. The truth of the present: Michele's present, Lewis's present, Rita's present, my present, and your present. The truth of the future: Michele's future, Lewis's future, Rita's future, my future, and your future.

Abe: Don't speak to me in riddles. That's all I hear from Lewis. And believe me, I hear enough from him.

Damon: You're wrong. You can never hear enough from him because he makes so much sense; more than any of us. As for riddles, one has to speak in riddles in order to understand another who speaks in riddles.

Abe: Tell me what you know, or . . .

Damon: Or what, Doctor? Are you going to report me to some board, some committee, and tell them . . . What would you tell them? I have an intern that has figured out the problem of a patient that I haven't been able to understand for more than twenty years. They would laugh in your face. Or let's say they believed you and called me in. I can just imagine it now.

At this point, all the lights are turned down, and a spotlight is focused on Damon. A second spotlight is focused on Dick Goldschmidt, head of the Committee of Investigative Affairs into unprofessional behavior by doctors on staff.

Dick: Damon, have you ever worked with the patient in question: Lewis Strange?

Damon: I have.

Dick: And what was your relationship to that patient?

Damon: I was his intern, and a hell of an intern at that, if I do say so myself.

Dick: Do you know the patient's problem, or anything relating to the problem that could help this fine doctor over here to do his work?

Damon: How could I? I am just an orderly. Personally, I think the doctor is frustrated and looking for an excuse.

Dick: Your personal comments aren't needed.

Damon: I'm sorry, sir. What I was trying to say is that if he has been studying a patient for more than twenty years, how could I, an intern, know the man's problem after twenty months? I like to think I have talent and a bright future, but let's face the truth. I simply don't have that much talent and ability at this point in my life.

Dick: Thank you. That is all. Sorry to have wasted your time.

Damon: Best of luck in the future. You are very wise.

The spotlights are turned off, and the stage is lit up. Once again, the audience is able to see Damon and Abe in the hallway. Lewis is still seated at a table on the left side of the stage talking to himself. Dick Goldschmidt exits the stage through the back.

Damon: Do you want to subject yourself to that kind of humiliation?

Abe: I don't think . . .

Damon: Imagine what would happen to your reputation. You would become the laughingstock of this hospital and, more importantly, the entire medical community. I think you should listen to my riddles, put them together, and solve them.

Abe: But why won't you just tell me the answer? Why won't you save him?

Damon: Because, as I said earlier, everyone in that room wants something. Michele wants her parents jailed, and she needs Lewis. Rita and yourself want to solve Lewis's problems and publish the results.

Abe: That's not true!

Damon: You know once you find out Lewis's problem, you and Rita will publish a book. I wouldn't be surprised if it is already written. And don't deny it, because you would be stupid not to. A book on Lewis Strange would generate all the money you would ever need. You would become the leading psychologist in the field of schizophrenic study. You would be able to pick and choose your patients instead of worrying about seeing two or three at a time. You would be able to study unusual cases in depth. If another Lewis came around, you would be able to spend twice as much time on him as you did on Lewis.

Abe: If you're worried about credit, we will include you.

Damon: Doctor, you don't understand. It is not about money, power, or even knowledge of the insane. It's about a human being that is nuts, crazy, insane, whatever you want to call Lewis. But that isn't even the reason I want to be involved. That isn't the reason I come to that room every day and attempt to discover the truth.

Abe: Why do you go then?

Damon: I go because I also want something. I want him to continue to be insane so that I can continue my research. He is the last case I need to study before I can publish my book. I also honestly don't think he wants to be saved. She won't let him. She will constantly remind him of his past, that one day in history where everything went wrong and nothing went right.

Abe: Who will continually remind him? His sister? His pet? His mom? His grandma? Who will continually remind him?

Damon: They all will, and none of them will . . . the people of the present that hold similarities with them will remind him.

Abe: What people?

Damon: This is the last clue I will give you. They all used him at one point in time or another. They all would use him again. Who does he have left?

Abe: People that use him.

Damon: Right. Therefore, if someone stops using him . . .

Abe: He might open up to them and let them into his imaginary world.

Damon: Or he may come out of his imaginary world back to reality.

Abe: It is a good theory, but I'm not sure . . .

Damon: What aren't you sure of?

Abe: I don't think it will work, because he doesn't know that I am using him, nor Rita, nor Michele, nor yourself.

Damon: That is a valid point . . . If there isn't anything else, I am still holding a job at this hospital, and I have to get back to work before I get fired.

Abe: That's all. Thank you.

SCENE 3

Setting:

Rita, Abe, and Michele are located in a room about the same size as the one Lewis lives in. There is a two-way mirror on the back wall of the room through which they can see Lewis and the contents of his room. It is from here that they can observe all his actions, while the mirror appears like an ordinary mirror to Lewis.

Near the back of the room, the audience can see a desk. It belongs to Abe. Papers are lying everywhere, including on the floor. There is a half-brewed pot of coffee sitting on the left side of the desk. Next to the desk, there is a bookshelf filled with books. There are three other bookshelves scattered along the side of the room.

The room is relatively well lit. Abe is standing nearest to the two-way window. He seems entranced by Lewis's stoic image. Meanwhile, Rita is sitting on his desk. Michele is pacing back and forth between Abe and Rita.

Rita: What else can we do, Abe?

Michele: I'm not sure we've tried everything . . .

Rita: We have tried everything! Drugs, psychological treatment, compassion, anger, memories, future opportunities, everything! Even that trick about your sister, his sister, didn't work. The fact that we showed him Sara will never be a part of reality no matter what he does, and still . . .

Abe: What's your point?

Rita: We can't heal him, and if we can't trick him . . .

Abe: That's right, we couldn't trick him! So what's your point?

Rita: I don't think . . .

Abe: What don't you think?

Rita: I just . . .

Abe: What are you trying to say?

Rita: I think . . . that . . .

Abe: I can't help you unless you communicate with me. We're teammates; therefore, I have to know what you're thinking.

Rita: I don't think . . .

Abe: Spit it out! I don't have all day to decode your blubber.

Rita: You won't like it.

Abe: I don't like this!

Rita: I'm not sure . . .

Abe: Say something or shut up!

Rita: I'm starting to support the theory, the belief, that Lewis Strange is incurable. . .

Abe: That's nonsense!

Rita: As I was saying, I'm starting to think that Damon was right.

Abe: Damon has never been right.

Rita: I told you that you wouldn't like it, but I'm starting to think that we are all fools to think we can cure him. We can't heal him, because I don't think he can be healed.

Abe: What? When did this happen? When did you have this profound revelation?

Rita: When I discovered whose patient he really is.

Abe: Michele, can you give us a minute?

Michele exits the room into the hallway.

Abe: I explained that. He's our patient. I was just excited. I made a mistake. I'm sorry . . .

Rita: No! You were right! I don't have the passion, the love for Mr. Strange that you have. When my day ends, I don't go to a computer or to a research book to discover something that we may have overlooked during the day. I go home to my husband and our two kids. Those are the people I really care for. Lewis has just become a common piece of work. I think no more of him than I do that cup of coffee on your desk.

Abe: You can't be serious . . .

Rita: I am. Every day, I show up, and he is sitting in the same spot. He doesn't move, and he doesn't change. The same babbling every day. To me, Lewis is the secretary that beats me to work and the temp that stays late to impress somebody.

Abe: What does this all mean?

Rita: I'm starting to believe that he can't be healed because I don't care . . . or at least, I don't care enough.

Abe: You have to care to spend as much time with him as you do.

Rita: That's what I'm saying. I did care once. When this all began, I thought he could be healed, but . . .

Abe: But what?

Rita: After you began to help take away the strain of the case, you relieved me of the case. You relieved me from a feeling of responsibility. I stayed on because I felt there was a legitimate chance to cure him. But now I see I was wrong. I was naïve. Lewis Strange will never be sane. He cannot be healed.

Abe: He can be healed! He can be treated! I know he can. I've watched him come to the brink of reality a multitude of times. We just need something to drive him over the edge, to stop him from playing that silly game in the fantasy and imagination. I thought Sara Strange was that key. I thought Michele Strange was that key. I was wrong on both accounts. They brought him far, but not far enough. But I know, there has to be something.

Rita: What else can there be? As you said, you've tried every trick that we thought could work. Every lasting memory that you could find. You even tried to convince him that he would be able to come out and have us all as friends. But that didn't work either.

Abe: It almost worked . . .

Rita: Don't you see! It's not about what you and I can do for him anymore. We've exhausted our physical options. We've done everything in our power, and he still hasn't come back to reality. You have to face the fact that we can't do it! No one can do it but Lewis himself. And he has been there so long that he may not even be able to anymore.

Abe: But there has to be something . . . something that will take him over the edge.

Rita: But, as doctors at St. John's Hospital, we can't afford to anymore. The press won't allow us to go over the edge. Or at least, not after that whole Scott Hopkins incident last year.

Abe: Don't bring him up again! There was nothing we could do for that man that we didn't do. We tried our damndest, and I admit we failed. But the point was that we did the work and put in the hours. He just chose not to allow that time to benefit his own well-being.

Rita: I can't help but wonder if it wasn't our constant badgering, our continual obsession for the truth of his past, and the push for him to come back to the real world that forced him to do it.

Abe: In other words, you are afraid of our past mistakes, and you don't want to have a guilty conscience in case it happens again.

Rita: When you put it like that, it sounds so cruel and spineless. I only mean that you have put your time in on this patient. Sooner or later, you are going to spend more time on the others and less on Lewis Strange. Eventually, you will term him a hopeless case. You will believe that indeed he can't be helped. Otherwise, he may end up being just another Hopkins. We can't change the past, but we can change the future.

Abe: That's what I'm trying to do. After Hopkins's suicide I was devastated, but I learned that it only meant one thing.

Rita: What?

Abe: It meant that we finally did reach him. The most realistic thing in this world is death, and he faced death head-on. It may not have been exactly what we were looking for, but it was a part of reality. And if he made an action in reality, he had to have been back . . .

Rita: But it doesn't mean he was sane! You know as well as I do that suicides are often done by people who aren't acting like themselves. People who commit suicide are out of their minds and, in a way, insane.

Abe: My point is that it is nothing that we can change. It is nothing we should beat ourselves up over. It happened a long time ago. It was the first time that we turned our backs on a patient, and I won't let it happen again.

Rita: But we did turn our backs. We pushed him to the brink of his insanity by attempting to make him sane, and then we turned our backs and he killed himself.

Abe: Do you ever think that he may have wanted us to turn our backs on him? That he was waiting for a moment throughout the treatment to kill himself? I mean, he did have the tools already prepared and hidden for any occasion that he felt he would need them. How do you know he didn't have a plan to kill us for prying into his life?

Rita: What?

Abe: Maybe he was afraid of our questions? Maybe we pried too much? Maybe we caused too much pain? Or maybe, just maybe, he was afraid that we were on the right track. Maybe he was afraid that he was days away from becoming healthy and whole once again. Maybe he saw us as reality. Maybe reality scared him too much, and he momentarily came back and we weren't there.

Rita: What are you suggesting . . . that you should have somehow forced your way into his mind and fed him the right actions? Do you think you should have led him by the hand and into reality so that he wouldn't have to face it alone? Face it, Abe, that is impossible. The patient will have to see reality on his own when he comes back, no matter when he comes back. Whether it is by himself in a cold, dark room or if it is in front of a group of doctors wearing white coats and talking about him, he will have to face reality on his own before anyone from reality can help him.

Abe: Yes, but if I could have made my way inside his mind, maybe he would have been better prepared for whatever he faced when reality struck him.

Rita: Abe, do you know there is only so far a point that you can go to, otherwise, you will also become insane?

Abe: But what if I went past that point? What if I went past the point of no return that we are lectured about in school every year of our training? Do you think I could have saved him?

Rita: It doesn't matter, because in the process you would have made yourself insane. I mean, I can't say that for sure, but I think if you would have entered inside the mind of Scott Hopkins, you would have destroyed yourself.

Abe: Do you think he would have been saved?

Rita: I don't . . .

Abe: Answer the questions!

Rita: Yes, but . . .

Abe: But nothing! Following logic like that means that I am responsible for Scott Hopkins's suicide. And I will be responsible for whatever happens to Lewis if I don't go past the point of no return.

Rita: Abe . . . that's insane! If you try to get inside his mind, you could become insane. I mean, it is a dangerous risk that you don't want to take. It could become fatal to your health.

Abe: But if I don't take this chance, my patient will surely remain insane.

Rita: That's not what's important!

Abe: You are wrong! That is the most important thing . . .

Rita: Abe . . .

Abe: Listen to me. I have a code of honor. I believe that I must do everything in my power to save my patients. I have made it my goal to make the unhealthy healthy. Just as a lawyer would have to release evidence whether it proved his client innocent or guilty, I have made a personal oath to myself to save my patients if the opportunity is there. The opportunity was once there, and

I ignored it. That patient is dead. I can't allow it to happen again. I will not have another loss of life be my responsibility.

Rita: Even if it is your life?

Enter Michele.

Michele: Is it okay to come back in now? Or am I interrupting something?

Rita: No. The doctor and I just finished discussing your brother's situation.

Abe: That's right. That's right. Your brother gets worse every day instead of improving. Each day, he is continuing to manifest the voices from the past. You heard Rita's feelings that he cannot be healed. I am inclined to think differently. Yet, this development of new voices scares me, because I don't understand it.

Michele: What do you mean you don't understand it?

Abe: It isn't right. We are giving him more treatment than we have ever given one single person, yet he is still able to develop these voices through the treatment. Medically, that isn't possible. He is defying every law that Rita and myself have ever seen with the mentally disturbed.

Michele: What does all this mean?

Abe: I'm not exactly sure what it means. That is what puzzles me. That's also why I want to talk to you later on today. We will go over his past like we have so many times before. There has to be some event, some occurrence that explains his case.

Michele: So I have to talk about the life I keep trying to forget?

Abe: Yes. I'm sorry to say that is the only chance we have in locating your brother's problem. You must tell me his story, your story, your parents' story, no matter how painful it is. You know, like we have always done.

Michele: I still don't understand why.

Abe: Because I want to think like he does. I want to know why he has so many emotions swirling inside his head. I want to know what society has done that he considers so awful.

Rita: Abe, I don't want you to do it. It's too dangerous.

Michele: Is that true? It's dangerous for you, Abe?

Abe: Yes, but it is the only way we can solve your brother's problems. It's the only way we can get inside his head.

Michele: I don't want you to do anything that will put you in danger.

Abe: It's my job to cure my patients. The only way I can cure this one is to understand how he thinks. In order to do so, I have to make some dangerous and radical moves. As long as you tell me the truth, I will be all right. But if you lie to me, I could be in danger.

Michele: So you are putting all your trust in my hands? You are giving me your life?

Rita: He is. As a matter of fact, the doctor is giving you his sanity.

Michele: I don't know about this . . .

Abe: Do you want your brother cured?

Michele: Yes.

Abe: This is the only method we have left to try and cure him.

Rita: I don't think it will work.

Abe: There is only one way to find out, and that's if we try.

Rita: But it is so dangerous.

Abe: Do you have any other suggestions?

Rita: No.

Abe: Then the decision is Michele's.

Michele: You say there is no other way to cure him?

Abe: That is correct.

Michele: And are you all right with risking your own personal safety for the health of my brother?

Abe: I am not at risk as long as you tell me the truth. As long as you can remember every conceivable detail that is important to Lewis's situation right now.

Michele: When do you want to do it?

Abe: I will let you know. Right now, I'm worried about my patient.

Abe turns toward the glass to speak to Lewis. Michele also looks at Lewis as Rita begins to speak.

Rita: Look, he's doing it again. Will he ever stop?

Michele: No. Not again.

Abe: He times it too well.

Lewis: No! That isn't true! Oscar was by the door! Oscar was the easiest to free! I didn't know where anyone was, but Oscar . . . Oscar was reliable. He was reliable. He was always in the same spot, and he was always there when I needed him. I had to save him!

Abe: We are here for you, Lewis. We are as reliable as Oscar. Why won't you realize that? Why won't you let us help you? Why won't you let me inside your mind? Michele, Oscar was his pet, right?

Michele: Oscar was his imaginary pet. He pretended to keep it by the door of the house.

Abe: What was it?

Michele: A dog.

Abe: Did it die in the fire?

Michele: No. He saved it instead of trying to save any of us. Could that be why he is like this?

Abe: It is a possibility. Who would have blamed him for saving Oscar?

Michele: Anyone. It could have been Mom, Dad, myself, Sara, Christian, or . . .

Abe: Or who?

Michele: Or Jilie.

Abe: Wait a minute. Who's Jilie?

Michele: Jilie . . . you mean . . . I have never told you about Jilie?

Abe: No.

Michele: How could I have been that stupid? How could I forget to tell you about Jilie?

Abe: Who was Jilie?

Michele: Jilie was an evil person. She was our housekeeper, and she watched us a lot as kids. In a way, she was a second mom to us. However, in reality, she was only a housekeeper, a nanny.

Abe: How did she treat you?

Michele: She loved me like I was her own daughter. She cared for me, fed me, punished me, made sure that someone was always there for me when I needed people to be there. Because, as I have told you before, my parents really didn't love any of us kids.

Abe: How did she treat the rest of the kids?

Michele: She was nice to all of us. She did the same for Christian and Sara, but Lewis . . .

Abe: What about Lewis?

Michele: Oh, Lewis . . .

Rita: What did Jilie do to Lewis?

Michele: Jilie always blamed him and his imaginary friends for anything that went wrong.

Abe: You mean Oscar?

Michele: No. All of his imaginary friends.

Abe: How many friends did he have?

Michele: You mean imaginary?

Abe: Yes.

Michele: I think about ten or so . . . I'm not exactly sure.

Abe: How come you never told me about this before?

Michele: I thought I had . . .

Rita: No, you didn't! How many real friends did Lewis have?

Michele: Two: myself and Dan.

Abe: He was hearing voices when he was that age . . . How old was that, exactly?

Michele: I'm not sure. I think he was six or seven.

Rita: Abe, this is what we have been looking for!

Abe: Don't get too excited. It is definitely a major piece of the puzzle, but we still don't know where it goes or how to fit it with the rest of the pieces.

Rita: I'm not sure I understand what you're saying.

Abe: There is still some more hidden information remaining. I think I may discover it later when I talk more with Michele. I know I have to be direct with my questions and stir her memories instead of holding the general conversations I have in the past. I still am very interested in this Jilie person. She is a piece of the puzzle . . . She has some kind of meaning . . . But she isn't the answer. Continue with your story, Michele. I want to hear more about Jilie.

Michele: There isn't much more to tell about Jilie, but I can tell you a story that explains her relationship with myself, Lewis, and the other children.

Abe: Let me hear it.

Michele: Well, when I was cooking, I accidentally dropped a match that caught fire to a paper towel. At first, I didn't realize it happened. Then I sat and watched it burn. It was like a disease that was crawling toward me. I wanted to run, but I was fascinated by it. The house was starting on fire, and I could only stare at the piece of paper. The orange, yellow, and red glow was so beautiful. It was a very peaceful moment even though it was a very dangerous one. Then Jilie came running in and saw the fire. She was screaming in a hysterical fashion. But at the same time, she held enough composure to find some water and put the fire out. Then she looked at me. I could see the rage in her eyes. She was ready to kill someone. After all, the house had almost burned down. She looked at me and said . . .

Abe: What did Lewis do?

Michele: How . . . did you know she . . . she blamed . . . Lewis?

Abe: Call it a hunch.

Rita: Either a hunch or he actually is starting to understand the problem. Aren't you, Abe?

Abe: Not now; I'm thinking. Now, what did she do to Lewis?

Michele: She grabbed him by the ear and dragged him around the kitchen, the living room, the whole fucking house! The entire time, she was screaming obscenities and calling Lewis an ungrateful, irresponsible little shit. Then she went insane. She started saying Lewis was stupid and his imaginary friends and animals were stupid. She even called him insane.

Abe: How did that affect Lewis?

Michele: Jilie didn't understand that Lewis thought these friends and animals were real. She didn't understand that her screaming was driving him mad. Then, as if she hadn't caused him enough pain . . .

Rita: What did she do?

Michele: She grabbed his wrist, holding his palm out into the air facedown. She took a lighter from her pocket . . . She held his hand above a lit lighter. It seemed like it lasted for hours. It looked so painful. His hand was burnt. No actually, it wasn't burnt. It was charred. If you look at his hand now, you can still see the scar or the burn mark, or . . . whatever you call it. She was so mean to him.

Abe: What did your parents do?

Michele: My parents had to take him to the hospital. Jilie got fired, but Lewis still got yelled at for hours by Mom and Dad. They said if he wouldn't have been so damned irresponsible, he wouldn't have gotten burned, and Jilie wouldn't have lost her job.

Rita: What happened to Lewis after that?

Michele: He got really weird. Jilie destroyed his love of fire. He completely stopped playing with matches, lighters, you know, anything related to fire.

Abe: What happened when he saw a real fire?

Michele: He would just roll up into a ball and hide. Then, he would mumble the same phrase over and over again.

Rita: What was the phrase?

Abe: I didn't do it.

Michele: That's right, but how did you know?

Abe: It doesn't matter.

Rita: So Jilie changed him?

Michele: Yes.

Rita: What kind of change was it?

Michele: Jilie made Lewis lose love of any kind. He was miserable in the real world. Then, he started to become distant. Or at least more distant than he had ever been before. It was almost as though he was in his own world.

Rita: What about his imaginary friends? What happened to them?

Michele: His imaginary friends seemed to increase, and he stopped talking to anyone but Sara, Christian, and Dan.

Rita: Did he still talk to you?

Michele: Occasionally, but he tried to avoid it, if it was at all possible.

Rita: So she was the cause for his turn . . . How could you forget to tell us about Jilie?

Michele: I thought you knew . . . I mean . . . I thought I mentioned it before.

Rita: Regardless, this is a huge step. It seems like we succeeded in finding another major piece of the puzzle, didn't we, Abe?

Abe: What?

Rita: Haven't you been listening?

Abe: I have. And I agree that this is a big step, a big piece of the puzzle, but it isn't enough . . .

Rita: It's more than enough! It explains . . .

Abe: It explains a lot, but it's missing something.

Michele: How can you say that?

Rita: We just located where the numerous personalities came from, and that allows us . . .

Abe: It allows us nothing. We located where the personalities started to increase and change. We still don't know why they began. We don't know why he holds onto some of the voices and gets rid of others. We don't know what purpose each voice serves.

Rita: Then what do we know?

Abe: We know that every voice is a manifestation of a voice from some point in his life. Now, we just have to figure out the significance of each voice in his life. We have to find out who his first imaginary friend was and where they came from.

Rita: That will take time.

Abe: Something that Lewis doesn't have very much left of, if you get what I mean.

Rita: Nor do we.

Michele: Why don't you have more time?

Abe: Remember the argument I was having with Rita when you entered the room?

Michele: Yes, but . . .

Abe: I'll get to that. As you know, we are licensed to do a job. We have many patients, and we have bosses. Although it appears that we are free to do what we want, we do have to follow a very tight schedule made by our superiors.

Michele: What does this have to do with Lewis?

Abe: There are people above us who believe that we have been spending entirely too much time on this case. They think we should give up and write him down as a lost soul, because this private institution is losing money.

Michele: What does . . .

Abe: That means that our superiors are telling us to stop spending time and money on an incurable patient. Rita has given her opinion that she is inclined to agree with their recommendation.

Michele: How can you do this?

Rita: I've been on this case since the beginning, and I don't think we can do anything more with him with the resources we have.

Abe: I agree with her that we don't have the resources we need. Lewis could use a third psychiatrist with some new ideas and perceptions of his situation. Then he might be cured.

Michele: Get him a third psychiatrist then!

Abe: It's not that simple. I told you, we need money. Our superiors are only going to start to allow for decreased time and attention. After a couple of weeks, he will be left to his imaginary world in a room with twenty other mentally disturbed people. Lewis will receive a weekly checkup and medicine. Other than that, he will eternally live in the imaginary world he loves so much.

Michele: What if I pay for you to spend more time with him?

Rita: You are paying.

Michele: What if I pay more?

Abe: It isn't that simple. Our bosses go for money. The next clients they have coming in are extremely rich. In the past, we have been able to keep Lewis because he created a constant amount of money for us every year. But these new clients . . . well, they can pay us in five weeks what we would make off of Lewis in five years.

Michele: What are you saying?

Abe: I'm saying that financially, our bosses think that there is a better option.

Rita: These new clients mean normal days for us once again. We will be able to see more of our families and less of Lewis's imaginary world. It sounds cruel, and it is. But we are human, and we do have lives outside of this hospital.

Michele: Is there any hope that Lewis will become healthy in the next two weeks?

Rita: No. *(at the same time as Abe)*

Abe: Yes. *(at the same time as Rita)*

Abe: I think I am beginning to understand his problem. If I can treat that problem, and it is, in fact, the problem, I will save him. But . . .

Michele: But what?

Rita: If Abe is wrong with whatever he is thinking, Lewis could end up eternally haunted by the voices and, therefore, he would always be like this.

Michele: Be like what? Say it, Doctor.

Rita: Insane.

Abe: I think it is time we have that talk about Lewis's past. We have missed a lot in the past, and we can't let that happen again. I want to know everything about Lewis. I want to know about his family, his friends, every detail. If I've ever heard it before, I want to hear it again. I've got to find some shred of information to get inside of his mind before it is too late . . . if it isn't already too late.

Rita: I'm not sure I like this . . .

The lights are dimmed, and the curtains close.

SCENE 4

Setting:

In an unusually crowded hallway near Lewis's room, the audience can see a man standing against the wall and keeping to himself. He is reading a paper and smoking a cigarette. As indicated by his name tag, the audience can see that his name is Seth. He is short and wears glasses. He also holds the annoying habit pushing his glasses as far back on his nose as they can go.

After a few moments, the audience sees Michele's stunning figure swagger past Seth. She makes a motion at Seth, and Seth responds with a similar motion.

Seth: Michele, I have to speak to you immediately.

Michele: Okay, what do you need?

Seth: Not here.

Michele: Why?

Seth: Trust me. Now, is there someplace that we can talk in private?

Michele: What do you mean?

Seth: Is there someplace we can talk where no one will be able to see or hear you?

Michele: Why?

Seth: Because you don't need to be seen by anyone around here when I tell you the news I have.

Michele: What do you mean?

Seth: I mean your reaction . . .

Michele: What is this nonsense?

Seth: This isn't nonsense, but I think you might not want anyone to see you when I tell you what I have to say.

Michele: Very well. In here.

Seth follows her into a room on the side of the hallway. The janitor sign can be read clearly on the door. Meanwhile, as Seth enters the room, he notices that there isn't very much space. As he closes the door, he realizes that he is chest to chest with Michele. The room is also very dark, as light from the hallway no longer invades the room. After a few seconds, Michele turns on a light that appears ready to be burned out.

Michele: Let me hear it.

Seth: Patience, let me . . .

Michele: I let you do nothing! What could be so important, yet so secret?

Seth: We discovered your parents' location, the names they are living under, and the names of the people that helped them hide from us for so long.

Michele: That's incredible news!

Seth: I'm just coming to the incredible part.

Michele: I'm not sure . . .

Seth: We found another witness. Someone else saw the fire and saw your parents fleeing.

Michele: How is that possible? Everyone else died . . .

Seth: This person wasn't in the house, and she wasn't a neighbor.

Michele: Who could have remained silent for this long? Who would have been so cruel to allow my brother to be the way he is for his entire life, and to allow me to live a life fleeing from my past?

Seth: Your grandma.

Michele: My grandma!

Seth: She is a remarkable lady, even at the age of ninety-two.

Michele: But why? Why would she wait so long? After all the conversations I had with her about Lewis . . . She knew the amount of pain that event caused me. She knew it drove Lewis into an entirely different world. Why would she allow that pain to continue if she had a chance to stop it?

Seth: Because even though she knew her daughter was wrong, she loved her. She couldn't let her lose the middle of her life in the corner of an empty, dirty jail cell.

Michele: So she let Lewis spend the better half of his life in a room full of doctors and voices that don't exist.

Seth: I'm not saying she was right. I'm just telling you what she told me, even if she came forward with this information on her own.

Michele: Why, this late in her life, after all that has gone on, did she decide to make amends? To tell the truth?

Seth: Because she is going to die.

Michele: What?

Seth: I wasn't supposed to say anything . . .

Michele: But you did. So tell me.

Seth: She has cancer. She has two weeks left to live. She wanted to clear her conscience before she dies.

Michele: Do you have her in custody?

Seth: We have everyone in custody. All we are waiting for is you.

Michele: What do you mean?

Seth: Any arrangements you might need to make. . .

Michele: I still don't understand.

Seth: Well. You are forgetting where you're currently at. Once you act, your role at the hospital will be done, and you will have to act like any other patient's relative.

Michele: No more up close and . . .

Seth: It will all be over. Lewis will be completely alone.

Michele: I want you to hold off a while. I still want to be around Lewis. Put my grandma under protection and lock my parents away.

Seth: They might get free if we don't act . . .

Michele: They won't. They've been on the run for over twenty years. They tried to kill their family and blame a child for the accident. No judge would let them go free, not until there was some kind of trial.

Seth: But why do you want to wait?

Michele: Because if I admit to all this, Abe and Rita will interview me and dismiss me. I won't be able to watch my brother. I won't be able to pretend I am investigating a case. I will be forced to leave Lewis alone. That's how the whole problem started. I left him alone. I can't do that again.

Seth: I didn't think you loved him?

Michele: But I do! I really do love him.

Seth: All right, but be careful. You don't want to do anything that would lose respect for Emma Kenda.

Michele: I know. But I also know what I am doing, and I will be all right.

Seth: Just remember. Life is short. You can't spend it all with Lewis, just because you weren't there for ten minutes.

Michele: I'll keep that in mind. Now, if that's all, I have a meeting with Abe.

Seth: Well, there is one other thing that I . . .

Michele: I have that meeting . . .

Seth: It's important!

Michele: Meet me later today.

Seth: When? Where?

Michele: I'll call you.

Seth: Sure.

Michele: Bye.

Michele exits the cramped room through a door on the opposite side from which she entered. Seth remains alone in the closet.

Seth: Bye. But be careful. If only you knew everything, Michele... The game is a lot more complicated than you think. If only you knew whose house your parents have been living at for the last twenty years or so. I don't yet understand why or how it fits in, but it explains why Lewis has never been healthy. It explains why Abe can't pull him out. If Rita weren't around, I believe Lewis would be walking around on the streets, and your parents would be in jail. Be careful.

SCENE 5

Setting:

On the right side of the stage, Damon, Rita, and Abe are gathered in Abe's office. Each of them appears to be puzzled as they watch Lewis through the two-way mirror. Meanwhile, on the left side of the stage, Lewis Strange sits alone and continues to speak to himself with the same words and the same actions that he has in the past.

Lewis: Nine . . . wait! I mean eighteen, I'm not sure . . . what year is this?

Damon: What is he doing now?

Rita: He doesn't even know his real name.

Abe: Do we?

Rita: Isn't it Lewis?

Damon: She's right . . .

Abe: No . . . I don't think it is!

Damon: Now you're crazy!

Rita: Damon!

Abe: Let me explain.

Rita: Go ahead, but you do sound, well . . .

Abe: Don't worry. I know how I sound, but I think Lewis is somebody he wanted to be.

Damon: I'm not sure . . .

Abe: Let me finish! I think too many people stopped him from being Lewis or tried to stop him, and that's why he assumed this identity.

Rita: Are you suggesting that this isn't Lewis Strange?

Abe: That is exactly what I am suggesting. I think Lewis Strange is another identity, another front to cover his true identity.

Rita: That's a good theory, but there is one major flaw.

Abe: Which is?

Rita: How do you explain the existence of Michele?

Damon: And the fact that she says his name is Lewis?

Abe: I can't.

Rita: There's no evidence, Abe.

Abe: I just have this hunch.

Damon: A hunch isn't scientific.

Abe: It may not be scientific, but then again, nothing scientific has ever worked with Lewis.

Damon: It just doesn't make any sense.

Abe: I know, but I just feel like I can feel this through Lewis somehow. It's almost like . . . like I'm inside his head.

Rita: This is why I don't think we will ever cure him.

Damon: What do you mean?

Rita: We keep having these problems with Lewis. He doesn't give us anything to go with. Then when he does tell us something important, he changes it the next time around. It is almost like this whole thing . . . I'm not sure anymore.

Abe: It's almost like the whole thing is a game to him.

Rita: And the consequence of his loss is a trip to reality . . .

Damon: I want to go back to the idea that Lewis is just another manifestation of a personality that this person idolized or hated.

Abe: What about it?

Damon: How would he be able to take on such an identity? What I mean is, how could his mind handle it?

Rita: And how does Michele fit that idea?

Abe: You will think I'm crazy if I continue to . . .

Rita: Abe, don't hold out on us. I've never thought you to be crazy in the past, and I never will think you're crazy.

Damon: Come on, Abe . . .

Abe: I have a theory that explains it all. I've been tossing it around in my mind for about six months. I've just been afraid to voice it, because it sounds crazy to me.

Damon: Spit it out!

Abe: I think it is easy to explain how Lewis's identity was able to take this form. Whoever Lewis Strange was in real life was the reason why Lewis became like this. He wanted so badly to have this person's life that he just took it. And before you say anything, think about the life he lives. A life of a child. He has no commitments, no problems, just the peaceful time playing in the fields with his best friend and sister.

Damon: What about Michele?

Abe: I think she doesn't know because it may have happened before she was born. Michele has always known him as Lewis Strange, but it could be that Lewis's parents just allowed him to adopt these ideas so that they wouldn't have to deal with the voices. However, what they didn't understand was that by allowing him to initiate the game, they allowed him to believe that he could switch personalities at any moment he wanted to in order to avoid his problems.

Rita: Seems a stretch, doesn't it?

Damon: I think it does.

Abe: Another explanation is that he could have been adopted. That is something that the parents could easily keep from the child and from their other children.

Damon: That's a more likely possibility and a very logical answer if Abe is right.

Rita: Why would they have done something like that to a child that young and not have explained what was going on?

Abe: I'm not sure. Like I said, these are just my hunches.

Damon: There is no proof.

Abe: Yet, somehow, I feel I am the proof.

Rita: What?

Abe: I feel that I am inside his mind, and I think there is a logical solution floating around somewhere.

Damon: But why? Why would anyone want to be this way?

Rita: Yeah. And why would anyone allow it to happen? Why wouldn't his parents have explained everything to him in order to help him maintain his true identity?

Abe: His parents probably didn't realize the problem was that bad until the voices began to show up.

Rita: That makes sense.

Abe: Then they probably were ashamed of their mistakes and didn't want the rest of the town scolding them.

Damon: Seems kind of selfish.

Rita: You'd be surprised at some of the selfish things people do.

Abe: Eventually, his parents probably just shunned him and took the attitude that he wasn't theirs in the first place.

Damon: That's cruel!

Rita: But very possible.

Abe: Remember, this is all theory. Or at least until I talk to his grandma and his parents.

Rita: Michele is looking for them.

Abe: As to why he would want to be this way, that is easy. It is my opinion that he wants to be the center of attention. Wherever he has gone, the world has always rotated around him. Even when he wasn't in church on Sundays, he was the center of attention because his dad tried the entire week to get rid of him. That feeling of being the center of attention has only continued as his life has developed. Now he has three doctors, a sister, and a police chief that stare at him constantly throughout the day. With each move he makes, he can make us all jump. He gets free food, free lodging, and he doesn't have to work. He can keep his identity as a child for the rest of his life. An identity he chose at the very beginning of his journey.

Rita: Do you really believe that a man would make up that much pain just to receive a little extra attention?

Abe: To him, it's not pain, and it's not made up. It's the way he made for himself to understand reality. The voices may be his way to avoid any pain that might exist or might arise within his life.

Damon: How do we prove if this theory of yours is right?

Abe: The key to discovering whether or not my theory is correct is to talk to his parents, grandma, and anybody else that was close enough to him to really know his true identity.

Damon: Shouldn't there be some sort of proof towards his identity?

Abe: What do you mean?

Damon: If he was adopted, there should be some records or something to indicate the adoption process.

Abe: I see what you're saying.

Rita: Is it possible to find those records?

Abe: It may be.

Damon: Wouldn't somebody have looked for them by now?

Abe: Not necessarily. No one has ever really cared to look for such things in the past, as far as we know. If they had existed, they could have been destroyed. The pastor had a lot of power in that small town. He was able to bury the arson file for a while. Compared to that, what's a few adoption papers?

Rita: The people who did this should be jailed!

Michele Strange enters stage right. She is dressed in blue jeans and a white sports coat. She is wearing cowboy boots, and her gun is lodged at her side once again.

Michele: If I have anything to say about it, they will be.

Abe: How long have you been there?

Michele: I just arrived. I was in the neighborhood with another case, so I decided to stop by. Why? Did I miss something?

Damon: Was Lewis adopted, by chance?

Michele: What? I don't know about him ever being adopted. Where did you come up with such a ridiculous notion?

Rita: It's only another theory. Crazy as it is, these two have concocted it to explain the reason for your brother's condition.

Michele: If he was, no one ever told me or any of the other kids in the family about it.

Abe: Is there any way you could get access to the files that might hold any such information?

Michele: That would be like searching for a needle in a haystack.

Abe: Yes, but can it be done?

Michele: Well . . . anything is possible.

Abe: Because it is a lot easier to search for a needle than nothing at all.

Michele: It would take a little work, but I guess that's what rookies are for.

Abe: Good. Now, I think it would be wise if we have that talk. There is a lot I need to know from you.

SCENE 6

Setting:

Abe and Michele are sitting in Rita's office at her desk. Abe is on the left side of the table while Michele is on the right side. The table has two cups of coffee from which steam can be seen evaporating.

Rita's office is very clean. There are a few file cabinets and one desk. Rita has also taken considerable time to decorate the office. There are elaborate paintings and pictures spread on the walls throughout the office. Meanwhile, plants also can be found sporadically throughout the room. There is a large picture behind Abe. The room is lit with sunlight.

Abe: Let's start at the beginning. How old was Lewis when your house burned down?

Michele: Twelve years old.

Abe: How old were you?

Michele: I was nine.

Abe: How old was Sara?

Michele: She was five.

Abe: Christian?

Michele: Who?

Abe: You mean you don't know a Christian?

Michele: I do, but there wasn't one in my family.

Abe: Lewis said there was.

Michele: He's also nuts.

Abe: Tell me about Christian.

Michele: Well, there isn't much to tell. He wasn't a close friend. As a matter of fact, I hardly ever saw him.

Abe: What was he like?

Michele: He was calm. He always seemed to have all the answers, even when other people seemed confused. He never lost his temper, and he never seemed to be flustered by any of life's problems.

Abe: So he was a very reasonable person who handled life's events in stride?

Michele: Exactly!

Abe: Interesting . . . all right, let's move on then. Who was Oscar?

Michele: Oscar was Lewis's imaginary friend.

Abe: Friend?

Michele: Well, Oscar was a dog, so it was more like he was Lewis's imaginary pet.

Abe: What did Lewis believe happened to Oscar?

Michele: Lewis still believes that Oscar is alive.

Abe: What about the fire?

Michele: Well, according to Lewis, Oscar was right by the door, so he had time to save Oscar from the fire.

Abe: Tell me more about the fire.

Michele: Like what?

Abe: Who started it?

Michele: I believe my parents started it with the intention of ridding us from their lives.

Abe: That's never been proven?

Michele: But it will be!

Abe: Don't get angry. I'm just trying to get the facts as Lewis would see them and as they really happened. Please continue telling me about the fire.

Michele: My parents were hoping that the fire could be blamed on Lewis and then they could commit him to an asylum for insanity.

Abe: So your parents were just after Lewis?

Michele: Not exactly. I think they were hoping we would die, and then the blame could fall on Lewis and they would be free of us all.

Abe: Without knowing what you know now, do you think it would have worked?

Michele: I can't say, but what I can say is that it would have been easy to pull off. I mean, Lewis had a reputation for playing with matches and starting fires. Everyone also heard him talk to those imaginary friends at some point in their lives.

Abe: Why did their plan fail?

Michele: Lewis came home early, and then he escaped after the fire started. I also escaped. Too many things went wrong for them for their plan to succeed.

Abe: Before Lewis escaped, did he try to save anyone?

Michele: Oscar was the only one that he attempted to save from the fire.

Abe: He didn't even try to save you or Sara?

Michele: My room was upstairs. There was no way he could have saved me had I been inside, so I understand why he didn't come after me. However, Sara's room was right next to where he kept Oscar.

Abe: So legitimately, he could have saved Sara instead of Oscar?

Michele: I wasn't there, so I can't say, but if I were in his shoes, I think I would have attempted to save Sara.

Abe: Were your parents ever caught or convicted?

Michele: They were caught once. I think it was somewhere in Montana.

Abe: Why weren't they brought up on charges?

Michele: Apparently, a woman helped them escape.

Abe: Who was this woman?

Michele: No one there knows. The only thing the fine police of Montana could tell me when I asked them about it was that the woman was helped by another woman.

Abe: So there were two of them?

Michele: Yes, and one of them was very, very old.

Abe: Interesting. Now, don't take the following question too harshly, but I have to know.

Michele: Don't worry about offending me. I'm a very hard person to offend.

Abe: How come . . . well, what I mean to say is why . . . why has Lewis suddenly become so important to you again?

Michele: Because he is my brother and . . .

Abe: No, I mean why is he important to the police search for your parents?

Michele: I'm not sure I understand.

Abe: Why do you have to spend every possible moment here, with the hope of talking to him if he slips back into reality?

Michele: Because he is the only remaining witness.

Abe: What about yourself?

Michele: My life depends on my identity. Nobody knows that I am Lewis's sister except for a few select people that work here, like yourself.

Abe: Why don't you become a witness and receive a new identity?

Michele: Because I have already changed my identity once. I don't want to change who I am and relocate again. Besides, I am the one who unburied the case. If I stop my involvement, I know the case will be buried again, and Lewis will be forgotten. My parents will go free. My life will be ruined. And Lewis will remain insane forever.

Abe: You don't really think people would try to bury this case again?

Michele: They have before, and they will again. I'm not sure who, but I know it will happen.

Abe: I see . . . Tell me about your grandma.

Michele: My grandma?

Abe: Yeah. What was she like?

Michele: Why do you need to know?

Abe: You claim that Lewis spent Sundays with her. Therefore, she had a lot of influence over him. That influence could translate into one of the reasons why Lewis is in his present condition.

Michele: Grandma, influential?

Abe: She could have been very influential. She could also be very important to Lewis. So tell me, what was she like?

Michele: She was . . . well . . . she was a grandma. She was old. She was always giving us presents and basically spoiling her grandchildren. I remember this one time, she came over and gave me a dollar, which at the time seemed like a lot of money.

Abe: What did you do for the dollar?

Michele: That's just it. I don't think I did anything. I just walked out to the driveway and greeted her with my mom. I think I may have helped carry her bags or something.

Abe: How did she treat Lewis?

Michele: She was mean to Lewis. She didn't want to admit that she had a grandson that was crazy. I even remember that same story I told you . . .

Abe: Yes.

Michele: Lewis had done exactly the same as me and didn't get anything for it. And if that wasn't bad enough, she pulled him aside and said something awful to him.

Abe: What did she say?

Michele: I don't remember exactly, but it was something like, 'I didn't get you a present because you are a lunatic. You have no sense like these other children.'

Abe: Other children?

Michele: Sara received the same as me.

Abe: Why did your parents allow her to take care of him if she acted this way towards him?

Michele: Because, she was the only one who would do it. Besides, if she had him, it meant that my parents didn't have to deal with him. I mean, after all, Lewis was an embarrassment to an established pastor like my father. They couldn't take Lewis anywhere without people laughing at him, at them. It hurt my dad's image to have a fool for a son.

Abe: Your dad was a preacher, correct?

Michele: Yes.

Abe: What about your mom?

Michele: Mom was a faithful housewife. She cooked, cleaned, watched the kids, and occasionally babysat on the side for a little spare cash. That's the only reason Lewis ever met Dan.

Abe: Dan was Lewis's best friend?

Michele: Yes.

Abe: Is it true that Dan also had an obsession with playing with matches and lighting fires?

Michele: Among other things. The three of us formed a close bond. We played in a field near my house all the time.

Abe: Why are you smiling all of a sudden?

Michele: Dan was my first romance. I smile when I think about him.

Abe: Did Lewis know?

Michele: Lewis never knew about it. Or at least, we thought he never knew about it. We always felt it would be best if he didn't know.

Abe: Why is that?

Michele: At that age, you don't want to find out your best friend is trading cooties with your sister.

Abe: Continue with Dan's obsession of fire.

Michele: Dan was evil when it came to fires. He burned anything he could, and he always talked Lewis into doing the same. I remember one time, we all lit cigarettes and smoked them. All Dan talked about was how it made him feel powerful to hold the fire in his hands. Then, Dan and Lewis put the cigarettes out on their shoulders.

Abe: Why did they do that?

Michele: They said the scar showed their trust and friendship forever. It was a bond of sorts. To my knowledge, it was the only bond Lewis ever formed with anyone who was real.

Abe: So, Dan was the one that got Lewis to start playing with fire?

Michele: Yes, but then something changed.

Abe: What do you mean?

Michele: Lewis took the obsession to another level.

Abe: Give me an example of one such time.

Michele: Well, we were playing near our fort a few weeks later. Lewis seemed dazed. I don't know if he was bored or if he wasn't there mentally. I will always wonder. What I do know is what I saw.

Abe: What did you see?

Michele: Lewis took some rubbing alcohol and poured it all the way up and down his right arm. Then he took a lighter and lit his arm completely on fire. But then instead of putting it out immediately like most people would, he let it burn. He just let it burn and stared at the flames. He seemed like he was in a trance. His eyes possessed a sort of love I had never seen him experience before, and I've never seen that look ever again.

Abe: Who put out the fire?

Michele: Eventually, Lewis put it out, but the fact that scared me wasn't the action itself.

Abe: What scared you then?

Michele: It was the fact that Lewis had Dan scared. You could see the fear in Dan's eyes. You could also sense that he was in awe of Lewis. Dan was nuts and he loved fire, but he would have never taken it to that level.

Abe: What happened to this love Lewis had?

Michele: Jilie.

Abe: Your housekeeper?

Michele: Yes. She was a cruel woman. She always made Lewis into a culprit and blamed him for anything that went wrong. Hell, she even blamed him for things that just happened.

Abe: Like what?

Michele: There was one time that she actually turned a hurricane into Lewis's fault. She told Lewis that all these people died because Lewis was being punished by God for playing with fire and talking to his imaginary friends.

Abe: How did she destroy Lewis's love for fire?

Michele: It was strange. She did exactly what made him love fire so much in the first place.

Abe: What do you mean?

Michele: Jilie took a lighter and held it to Lewis's palm until his palm was burned severely. After that, he never played with fire again.

Abe: Is that why you feel so guilty?

Michele: I'm not sure I understand where . . .

Abe: The fact that you were the one who started that kitchen fire, not Lewis. You were the reason he was punished, and even worse, punished severely.

Michele: No. My guilt lies with leaving him alone after the fire. If someone would have been with him, I mean, if somebody who cared about him would have been with him, maybe he wouldn't be the way he is.

Abe: What about Sara? Lewis had a special bond with her, didn't he?

Michele: Yes.

Abe: Why didn't he save her from the fire, especially with her room being so close?

Michele: I'm not really sure, because he has never been sane since. I wish I knew, but I don't. For all I know, he could have tried.

Abe: A few more questions and we will be done.

Michele: Okay.

Abe: What is Lewis's obsession with Abe Lincoln?

Michele: I'm not sure I know what you mean?

Abe: From time to time, he will identify Abe Lincoln. It's almost like he thinks he is in front of the Lincoln Memorial. Did that monument hold any special significance to him?

Michele: Not that I know of.

Abe: Has Lewis ever been there?

Michele: I don't think so, but I can't say for sure.

Abe: I think that about finishes it. Thank you.

Michele: No. Thank you for being the first person to ever really care about my brother.

Abe: Michele, you've been an important factor in his recovery. You have sacrificed a lot of time to do whatever you can to aid his mental health.

Michele: I've done what I could.

Abe: You've done more than that. You are in here more than anyone else. You are not here because it's your job like you often pretend. I know that. I understand that you love your brother and that you care deeply for him. I don't mind that you are also working while you're here, under one condition.

Michele: Which is?

Abe: Always be honest with me, and I will turn my cheek from the fact that you're disturbing a hospital by doing police work in its facilities.

Michele: Thanks, Doc. You don't know how much pleasure you give me by saying that.

Abe: Believe me, the pleasure is all mine just to have known you. Now, if you would excuse me, I am going to try to go help your brother.

Michele: Doctor . . .

Abe: Yes?

Michele: There is something I haven't told you. Today, just before I talked to you, one of my deputies alerted me to the fact that we have another witness in this case. It seems she was there that day. She saw the whole thing.

Abe: You mean to tell me that . . . Why didn't you tell me this earlier?

Michele: I was afraid I wouldn't be able to be around Lewis anymore. I don't want to be separated from him again.

Abe: I won't let that happen. Who is this lady?

Michele: My grandma.

Abe: Your grandma was . . . This could be good for Lewis. I may need to speak to her.

Michele: Let me know a time, and I can arrange for you to come down to the precinct and talk to her.

Abe: Great. I'll let you know . . .

Abe exits the room through the door opposite the window. Meanwhile, the lights begin to dim, and a spotlight is turned onto Michele.

Michele: Why can't we save him, God? Why did you have to scar him like this? Why do you have to make him a freak that is on exhibition for Abe, Rita, and Damon? Why can't you just let him be happy?

Meanwhile, in the hallway outside Rita's office, a spotlight is shown upon Abe as he mutters to himself.

Abe: Thank you, God. Michele was a bigger help than she ever has been before. I can see inside his mind. He is savable. All I have to do is make contact with him. His grandma is the piece of the puzzle I've been waiting for. She can help, but she isn't entirely the answer. The problem lies deeper than that. It lies with Sara, Jilie, Christian, and some unknown other. All I have to do is figure out why he keeps talking to Abe Lincoln. Is he feeling what I'm thinking? Does he know that I am sneaking into his mind? Am I Abe Lincoln in his fantasy world? That's too far-fetched an idea, but he does seem more open with me when we are alone.

The lights are dimmed completely, and the curtains are closed.

SCENE 7

Setting:

Abe stands in the corridor of the asylum outside Lewis's room. The hallway is dark, with the exception of some red light that reflects through the hallway from the Exit sign. Through this light, the audience can see the clock over his head, which shows that the time is just after midnight.

Abe: I know this is wrong, but the riddles point here. My mind tells me that this is the only move. Lewis wants a friend, one that is real and not just a memory from the past. I hope Rita and Damon can forgive me for what I am about to do. I know this goes against all my professional ethics, but I have to do this. If not for Lewis, for myself. I have to talk to him alone so that I can see inside his mind. He knows when Rita, Damon, and Michele are in the room with me. He doesn't want to tell them, but he wants to tell me. I am his only friend. I am the only one who really cares.

Abe places his hand on a scanner and then slides an identification card through a slot on the wall. The door opens, and Abe enters a room that is pitch dark. Abe cannot even locate Lewis until he starts speaking. It is also at this time that a spotlight is shown on each character when they speak.

Lewis: Why has everyone, everything, disappeared?

Abe: It's nice when there isn't any light.

Lewis: What?

Abe: I was never much of a fan of the light. I always preferred darkness. The light always seemed to distract me from what I wanted to do.

Lewis: I like the light. I want to follow it when my life ends, but I'm not sure I know how.

Abe: What do you mean? You have talked of the light in the past and seemed to understand it. Why do you doubt your knowledge?

Lewis: I'm not sure . . .

Abe: Did someone teach you not to understand the light?

Lewis: No. No one has ever taught me about the light! Or, at least, no one taught me properly. I lived with a pastor for years, but he never showed me the light. He wasn't kind enough to show me the way.

Abe: You mean you lived in the darkness your entire life?

Lewis: Yes.

Abe: You've been alone.

Lewis: Yes.

Abe: You know the dark.

Lewis: Yes.

Abe: You want to see the light. (*No answer.*) Do you want to see the light, Lewis?

Lewis: Yes. The dark is so ugly.

Abe feels around the wall and locates a light switch. He flicks it to the on position. After a few moments, a light flickers on, and the room becomes bright. All spotlights are turned off at this point.

Lewis: The dark is so ugly.

Abe: I disagree. I find the dark beautiful at times. It allows me to relax and examine my thoughts. It takes away the stress. That's why I wanted you to sit in the dark. I wanted you to examine your thoughts and relax.

Lewis: That's the problem. My thoughts add more stress than they relieve.

Abe: Yes, but if you control your thoughts, the darkness is a wonderful place.

Lewis: I understand. I found the darkness beautiful at first, myself. I even enjoyed it, but then . . .

Lewis appears dazed for a moment. He stops speaking and stares at the audience. After a few moments, he regains his thoughts and begins speaking once again.

Lewis: The darkness was beautiful, until I discovered that once you go in, you can never escape.

Abe: You can escape anytime you want to by turning on the lights.

Lewis: You don't understand.

Abe: What do you mean?

Lewis: The darkness grabs hold of you and possesses your soul. Then it possesses your mind. Once you enter, it is very difficult to step back, and then . . .

Abe: Then what?

Lewis: Then it controls you and doesn't allow you to leave. I didn't want to enter the dark, but someone talked me into it.

Abe: Who talked you into entering the darkness?

Lewis: That's not important!

Abe: What's important then?

Lewis: The important fact is that I entered the darkness. And, once I entered it, I became addicted.

Abe: What do you mean addicted?

Lewis: I had to have it all the time.

Abe: How so? I'm not sure I . . .

Lewis: First, it was my family. Then Oscar. Then Dan. Then the church. I couldn't resist. I tried to stop. I really tried to stop, but it was useless. The further I got into the darkness, the more I had to have it. It held so much control over me . . .

Abe: Who made you enter it?

Lewis: I'm not sure.

Abe: Was it your father?

Lewis: I don't know.

Abe: Was it your brother?

Lewis: I'm not sure.

Abe: Was it your therapist?

Lewis: I'm not sure.

Abe: Was it the politician?

Lewis: I'm not sure.

Abe: Was it Oscar?

Lewis: I'm not sure.

Abe: Was it Abraham?

Lewis: I'm not sure.

Abe: Was it your mother?

Lewis: I'm not sure.

Abe: Then who was it?

Lewis: I think it was all of them. They scared me. They all wanted me to do things that I didn't want to do. That's why I did everything opposite of what they said. I avoided them because I was afraid of what they had to say.

Abe: Are you still controlled and possessed by the darkness?

Lewis: I don't want to lose your support. I hate lying to you.

Abe: You won't lose my support!

Lewis: But . . .

Abe: Are you controlled and possessed by the voices?

Lewis: I'm not sure if I'm controlled by them or it.

Abe: An honest answer . . . How would you know if the darkness no longer controlled you? Or if the voices no longer possessed you?

Lewis: That's easy. If I didn't hear your voice and I was still able to see you, I would know I was all right.

Abe: When do you think you will find the light, Lewis?

Lewis: I'm not sure. I'm going to continue looking. I'll talk to you later.

Abe: Lewis! Don't go! . . . No! . . . Lewis! . . . Please don't go!

Lewis's face suddenly appears vacant and white. Abe appears to be in excruciating pain as he hits his head against the table screaming that he just needs a few more minutes. After a few moments, he rises and retreats from the room. As he is leaving, he stops and stares at the light switch. A few moments pass, and Abe flicks the switch. The lights fade out, and the curtains close.

SCENE 8

Setting:

Rita stands in the corridor of the asylum outside Lewis's room. The light reflecting off the Exit sign shows the time to be ten minutes after one.

Rita: Lord . . . help my soul. I have made some awful mistakes, and I am sorry, but . . . but I can't go back. My life depends on maintaining those mistakes from the past. Now, I have to know . . . I have to know what he knows, so I can expand upon my mistakes or end them now. If he knows nothing, I will be happy. Everything will be all right and people can get their lives back. But . . . if he knows something . . . I will be forced to take action. I will have to protect myself. I will be forced to protect them. Lord, I pray for this, for my own health, but I am also praying for his health. You must help Abe. He is determined to save someone who just can't be saved. Give Lewis the strength to let Abe help him. I don't want Abe to become another Lewis. It wouldn't be fair. It wouldn't be right. Help them help me. Most of all, forgive me and understand that this is done in the interest of everyone's health. The truth does not need to be known. It will do more damage than good.

Rita scans her ID through the door as she places her palm on the platform for identification. After passing through the security system, she enters the room and feels along the wall. After a few clumsy moments in the darkness, she finds her way to the light switch. The entire time this is occurring, she can hear Lewis talking to himself.

Lewis: Remember, I don't go to church! I don't believe in God! I don't follow those commandments because you teach them! Maybe someday, I'll find a Father who cares! And then I will follow those commandments!

Rita: (*Talking to herself.*) He's talking to his father again. Why won't that voice leave him alone? I hate to think that I am the only reason this continues, but . . . Abe is the only one who can help.

93

Lewis: I follow no religion! Jilie follows no religion! Oscar follows no religion! . . .

Rita: (*Again to herself.*) This is my chance to talk to him, to take control of the situation. He needs a guide, and I can guide him . . . I know where to lead him to . . . Or, at least, I know how to bring him to the world I want him in mentally. (*Rita speaks out loud.*) That was a mistake!

Lewis: Who are you?

Rita: I'm your therapist. My name is Clare.

Lewis: But your name tag says Rita.

Rita: My name is Clare. The name tag is a disguise so no one in the building will know that I snuck away to see you. I could get in big trouble for speaking to you.

Lewis: I know.

Rita: How's that?

Lewis: Well, everyone can get in trouble for speaking to me.

Rita: Why's that?

Lewis: Because they think I'm crazy.

Rita: Are you?

Lewis: You know I'm not, otherwise you wouldn't be here.

Rita: What was that?

Lewis: Nothing, I was just mumbling to myself. I do it all the time.

Rita: I know. Now . . . what's my name?

Lewis: Rita.

Rita: Lewis, my name is Clare.

Lewis: Then why does your name tag say Rita?

Rita: It's a disguise to confuse those who don't understand our relationship. After all, you don't want me to get in trouble for talking to you.

Lewis: No. I don't want you to get in trouble. Otherwise . . .

Rita: Otherwise, what?

Lewis: I'm not sure.

Rita: Now, let's start again. I want to know your name.

Lewis: Lewis Strange.

Rita: When were you born?

Lewis: A long time ago.

Rita: How old are you?

Lewis: I am nineteen.

Rita: How can you be nineteen if you were born eight years ago?

Lewis: Wait . . . I was born nineteen years ago! Now, I remember it clearly. But what happened to the past eleven years? Where have I been for that period of time?

Rita: Let's start again. What is your name?

Lewis: Jilie.

Rita: I thought you were Lewis?

Lewis: No, I didn't!

Rita: I see . . . Where are you from?

Lewis: I don't know. Where do you want me to be from?

Rita: When were you born?

Lewis: That's easy, but I can't tell you.

Rita: Why? (*No answer.*) Why can't you tell me?

Lewis: Because then Lewis will know.

Rita: What will Lewis know?

Lewis: That my name is Dan.

Rita: Dan, please let me talk to Jilie.

Lewis: Jilie got tired of this game. She went to play with Dan.

Rita: I thought you said your name was Dan?

Lewis: I was Dan, a long time ago. I'm hungry. I want to eat.

Lewis appears dazed and confused. His eyes roll, and his face seems to lose all expression. This appearance gets stronger as Rita continues to speak.

Rita: You can't eat until you tell me what happened that day. I have to know what you know, Lewis. I have to save your parents, myself, yourself, and Abe. I can't allow Abe to become what you have been your entire worthless life . . . Lewis, are you still there?

When Rita finishes speaking, Lewis rolls his eyes again, and all of a sudden he seems to be alert. He sits up in his chair and starts speaking.

Lewis: I have to go home for dinner and get some food. Then I can play. Then we can go to the park and shoot my BB guns at those squirrels.

Rita: Are you all right? Shit! I lost him again. I failed. I failed myself, Abe, Lewis, his parents, Michele, and all those who are like Lewis. I don't even know that he knows. I could be out of here as soon as tomorrow, or I could be here another thirty years. I can't take it anymore. My whole life depends on somebody that may or may not know he can destroy it. Why couldn't I find out what I need to know? I better get out of here before someone finds me. And some other night . . . some other night, Mr. Strange. You and I will meet again, and I will have to do what I don't want to do. It is something that will destroy yourself, Michele, and Abe. But it is something I have to do in order to save your parents, your grandma, and myself.

Rita heads toward the door. She opens it and turns out the light. Therefore, she can barely be seen in the red light reflected from the Exit sign as she speaks to Lewis.

Rita: Until we meet again, Lewis, the hospital will no longer be a safe place.

Rita lets the door shut behind her as she enters the corridor. As the door closes, all remaining light is blocked off. The curtains close.

SCENE 9

Setting:

Damon stands in the corridor of the asylum outside Lewis's room. Once again, as in the scene before, the clock can be seen through the reflection of the red light from the Exit sign. The clock shows the time to be a little past two. Damon is accompanied by two large men dressed in black suits.

Damon: I have to see Lewis. He is the key. Without him, my book will never be published. The facts won't be strong enough, and they won't be convincing. I won't get the freedom, money, and power I deserve. Abe is smart. He will figure the riddles out soon. There is little time left, and this is my only chance. It will be my only chance for the rest of Lewis's case. This is my last opportunity to speak to him alone. This is my last chance to confuse him once again. This is the last chance I will have to prolong his case and get the information I so desperately need for my book. If only she would leave him alone. She has been fouling up everything from the beginning and making the effects of his disease irreversible. I tried to get him to see that, but . . . he is blind at the moment. I've done all I can without ruining my chances. I can't afford to ruin my future. If Abe isn't careful, he will ruin his future. I warned him that Rita will eventually . . . that doesn't matter as long as he is careful . . . If he does solve the riddles . . . he will ruin Rita forever. He will ruin the future of Lewis's parents. I made the right choice. I saved four lives and cursed three. I only hope that when this all becomes public knowledge, the fact is understood that as a psychiatrist, I attempted to help the majority of the people and left the minority to face their own downfall. Someone will see me if I don't hurry . . .

Tank: Boss, who are you talking to?

Damon: Shut up! I told you not to speak. Now get ready. You and Ox, follow me through when the door opens. But remember, don't say a word when you're in there. Your only job is to keep Lewis from attacking me.

Tank: Right, boss.

Ox: Understood.

Damon places his hand on the scanner and runs his card through the reader on the door. The door opens and Tank, Ox, and Damon enter the room. Immediately, Damon flicks the light switch on and walks toward the table. He sits beside Lewis.

Damon: Lewis! . . . Are you there? Lewis! You are there, aren't you? . . . Lewis! . . . Where are you? (*Lewis remains silent.*)

Damon: Lewis! Listen to me! I am your therapist . . . I am your friend. Please, if you can hear me, give me a sign so that I know to stay. Otherwise, I will be forced to leave and see my other patients. (*Lewis's eyes open and shut numerous times.*)

Damon: What's your name? (*Lewis now closes his eyes.*)

Damon: I want to know your name . . . (*Damon is cut off when Lewis spits in his face.*)

Damon: I want to know your name immediately, or I will be forced to allow these two men to restrain you again!

Lewis: Fuck off! . . . I want to speak to Clare.

Damon: Who is Clare?

Lewis: Clare is my therapist.

Damon: No, I am your therapist.

Lewis: I want Clare!

Damon: Who is Clare? You never told me about Clare before. Was she part of your family?

Lewis: Clare is my therapist.

Damon: No! I am your therapist.

Lewis: Clare is my therapist!

Damon: Lewis, what's my name?

Lewis: Clare's my therapist!

The audience can see Lewis begin to rise from his chair. However, he is immediately forced to sit down by the two men next to Damon.

Damon: No! Rita is your therapist. I am your therapist. Clare is a friend of yours that neither of us have met, and we both would be honored if you introduced her to us.

Lewis: No! Only I can talk to my therapist.

Damon: I am your therapist! Now, what is my name?

Lewis: Clare is my therapist . . . Clare is my therapist . . . Clare is my therapist . . .

Damon: Fine! Clare can be your therapist, but then, who am I?

Lewis: You're Damon!

Damon: Good. How do you know me?

Lewis: You're my therapist.

Damon: Is it all right for me to speak with you and ask you some questions?

Lewis: You may, but whom do you want to speak with?

Damon: Can I please speak to Clare?

Lewis: No! Nobody speaks to Clare but me.

Damon: Fine. I would like to speak to Lewis. Is that okay?

Lewis: I think that can be arranged.

Damon: Who is Clare?

Lewis: A friend.

Damon: Is she a good friend?

Lewis: No. She is just a friend who understands me and always listens to me.

Damon: Does she ask you questions?

Lewis: Yes.

Damon: What kind of questions?

Lewis: What my name is, where I come from, what I do. You know, the standard, boring stuff. Nothing of interest.

Damon: Can I ask you some of that boring information?

Lewis: I suppose.

Damon: What is your name?

Lewis: Dan.

Damon: What do you do?

Lewis: I burn things.

Damon: Why?

Lewis: Because Jilie tells us to.

Damon: Who's Jilie?

Lewis: I am Jilie.

Damon: I thought you said you were Dan?

Lewis: No. Dan's dead . . .

Damon: How did Dan die?

Lewis: He burned to death at a church.

Damon: What was he doing at a church?

Lewis: Confessing.

Damon: What was he confessing?

Lewis: Attempting to murder Oscar.

Damon: Anything else?

Lewis: No.

Damon: You sure?

Lewis: Yes! Why?

Damon: Because, in the past, you told me that he was confessing to murdering your family.

Lewis: No. I told him that was all right. I understood why he did it. I forgave him. But the fact that he had murdered Oscar . . . that was wrong. That was the sin he had to confess.

Damon: Who's Oscar?

Lewis: Jilie will tell you.

Damon: I thought I was talking to Jilie.

Lewis: No. You were talking to Lewis.

Damon: Who am I talking to now?

Lewis: My name is Clare.

Damon: Clare, what do you do?

Lewis: I heal people.

Damon: What do you heal them from?

Lewis: Mental insanity.

Damon: How old are you?

Lewis: Thirty.

Damon: How old is Lewis?

Lewis: Forty-seven.

Damon: But he claims to be eight?

Lewis: He doesn't want to remember.

Damon: Remember what?

Lewis: His past.

Damon: What happened in his past?

Lewis: I can't tell you confidential information. You know that, Doctor.

Damon: How long did you treat him?

Lewis: Eleven years.

Damon: Then what happened?

Lewis: He appeared sane, so I let him go.

Damon: Was he sane?

Lewis: I think he might have been sane because all our conversations seemed to be games to him, but I don't know. He doesn't know. And honestly, after talking to Dan, I never want to know . . .

Damon: Who was Dan, exactly?

Lewis: You haven't met him?

Damon: We've met, but . . .

Lewis: You mean Lewis didn't introduce you properly? That ought to be changed. Dan . . .

(*Lewis stops talking.*)

Damon: Talk to me! Introduce me to Dan! . . . I know he holds the answers! He holds the future of the Strange family as well as the Adams family! . . . I am a friend! I can help! . . . I want to help! I have information for my book, and now all I want to do is help . . . Please, let me help.

Damon appears to be in tears, while Lewis has started into an entirely new conversation with no one in particular. Damon, Ox, and Tank look at him one last time, and then they begin to leave the room. Damon is the last one to the door, and he turns off the light before he exits. The lights go out, and the curtains close.

SCENE 10

Setting:

The stage is split into two sides. On stage right, Lewis Strange can be seen sitting at the table by himself. He is talking quietly, and throughout the scene, he becomes loud enough so that the audience can hear him.

On stage left, Abe, Rita, Michele, and Damon are sitting in Abe's office. Michele is sitting on Abe's file cabinet and talking to Abe as he paces the floor in front of her. Rita and Damon are standing closer to the door and are also engaged in a conversation. Both conversations can be heard by the audience. However, Abe and Michele cannot hear Rita and Damon's conversation, and vice versa.

Abe: Michele, no matter how much it pains me to say this, I think we might lose Lewis to his . . .

Michele: No! I'm not going to let that happen!

Rita speaks to Damon.

Rita: It isn't like Abe to give up so easily.

Damon: I agree. It is very unusual and illogical, but I will never try to understand him. Abe is his own person. He has his own personality.

Rita: Unlike Lewis.

Damon: Exactly, but since Abe said he was going to get inside Lewis's mind, he's been acting differently.

Rita: How do you mean?

Damon: It's hard to put your finger on, but there's been something unusual about him. Something strange . . .

Rita: I think I know what you're talking about. There has been something different about him lately, but he's still acting the same as he always has. It's almost as if the changes are so minute that only people who are close to him would notice them.

Damon: You mean people like us.

Rita: Well, he has no family.

Damon: I don't know him as well as you do, but it's almost like he's making the changes on purpose. It's like he knows what he's doing . . .

Rita: Or at least he thinks he does.

Damon: Do you think he knows about these changes in his attitude and personality?

Rita: No . . . and I don't think he wants us to know. Or at least, I don't think he wants us to realize that he has made changes . . .

Damon: Exactly, it's as if he's trying to hide something . . .

Rita: You mean like Lewis?

Damon: Exactly!

Meanwhile, Abe is still consoling Michele about the idea that she might lose Lewis.

Abe: I understand. It is hard, but Rita has been telling you that this has been a possibility all along. No one has ever lied to you and said there was no chance he would remain insane forever. Because the truth is that the chance has always existed for Lewis to remain insane.

Michele: But I didn't believe the two of you!

Abe: Why was that?

Michele: Because you were so confident. Rita wasn't, but you were. You seemed so smart, and you seemed to care more for him than anyone else ever has.

Abe: But I did always remain a skeptic.

Michele: I guess . . . at least . . .

Abe: At least what?

Michele: At least you tried. I guess I was just being naïve.

Abe: It isn't naïve to wish for a loved one to be healed.

Michele: I know. It's just . . .

Abe: What?

Michele: It's just, well, Lewis isn't the only one who doesn't want to face reality.

Abe: How so?

Michele: I know I've been avoiding the reality of this situation for the past few years. I've been avoiding the fact that my brother is insane and there is no way I can heal him. He is lost forever.

Abe: He's not lost. He was lost when you couldn't find him. At least you know where he is now, so if he ever does come back to reality, you can be there for him.

Michele: I know, but it's not the same. Knowing that my parents got away with this horrid thing . . . They destroyed his life and made me live an entirely different one than God intended for me.

Abe: Yes, but with your grandma, you now have a witness, and they will be punished.

Michele: Not exactly.

Abe: What do you mean?

Michele: The phone call came an hour or so ago. Grandma had a heart attack and died. Lewis and myself are once again the only witnesses.

Abe: I guess you'll have to testify.

Michele: Why? They don't know who I am. I'm not in danger. Lewis is happy where he is. Why would I want to risk my life to put them in prison for a few measly years?

Abe: For justice.

Michele: That wouldn't be justice. It would be more of a crime. The more I think about it, I've been hiding from reality with Lewis for the past few years. Now that I know he isn't coming back, I have to face it alone.

Abe: You're not alone.

Michele: Oh, I'm alone, and the reality is that my parents will run free. Lewis will die a slow, painless death in a room talking to voices of friends and family that no longer exist. And I . . . I will die a slow, painful death knowing that my parents got away with one of the cruelest crimes in the history of this century.

Abe: I will let you talk to him one final time, when I finish with him . . .

Michele: No! I don't want to be the last face he will ever see. I want to speak to him by myself. Then I will leave. Rita, Damon, and yourself can seal him in that room for the rest of eternity.

Abe: Are you sure?

Michele: This is the only way I can do it. I want my brother to be happy for the rest of eternity, instead of having to remember reality as something that was always trying to creep into his mind.

Abe: Then, the only thing I can say is I'm sorry, and the room is yours.

Michele: Thanks.

Abe: We'll clear out of this room so that you and Lewis can have one final private moment.

Michele: No. I appreciate the gesture, but I want you to watch. I'm going to sing him a lullaby that we used to sing together as children. See if you can notice anything important in his reaction.

Abe: I'm not sure . . .

Michele: It's my last chance, Abe! Look for anything. A twitch of the eye. A move of the arm. Anything! I want to give him one final chance before we all abandon him for the rest of his life. He's had a rough life, and I don't want to abandon him without doing everything in my power to save him. You know, I already abandoned him once . . .

Abe: I'll give it everything I have. I'm sure Damon and Rita will do the same.

Michele exits the mirrored room and walks around the back of the stage so that she can enter Lewis's room. The lights are turned off, and a spotlight is focused on her as she gets ready to enter Lewis's room.

Michele: Lord, please let him remember the lullaby. Let it bring him back. It is the only thing that hasn't been tried, and I want my brother back.

The lights are raised. Abe can be seen standing near Rita and Damon in Abe's office. They are all staring through the glass window in complete silence. No words are exchanged, because there are none left.

Michele: London bridge is falling down . . .

Lewis: Who's there?

Michele: Falling down. Falling down. London Bridge is . . .

Lewis: Where are you?

Michele: Falling Down. Falling down. Falling down . . .

Lewis: I loved that park.

Michele: London Bridge is . . .

Lewis: I loved that fort.

Michele: Falling down. Falling down. Falling down . . .

Lewis: The butterflies and fireflies were always there. They would play with me.

Michele: London Bridge is . . .

Lewis: I remember playing war, diving in the mud, and feeling the comfortable scrape of the weeds against my face.

Michele: Falling down. Falling down. Falling down . . .

Lewis: We pretended we were soldiers fighting in a war in a foreign country. We hid in a fort . . .

Michele: London Bridge is . . .

Lewis: The fort was great. Nobody bothered me there.

Michele: London Bridge is . . .

Lewis: But why did I paint it in orange and red?

Michele: Falling down. Falling down. Falling down . . .

Lewis: And why did we build a second one in the tree across from it?

Michele: London Bridge is . . .

Lewis: Those steps . . . Dan built them, but . . .

Michele: Falling down. Falling down. Falling down . . .

Lewis: That singing is so annoying. Why won't she shut up? Why won't she finish the song?

Michele: London Bridge is . . .

Lewis: I should ignore her, but I can't. Why can't I ignore her?

Michele: Falling down. Falling down. Falling down . . .

Lewis: How come I had forgotten about that fort? And why did I paint it orange and red?

Michele: The London Bridge is . . .

Lewis: Three of us built it. There was Dan, myself, and . . .

Michele: Falling down. Falling down. Falling down . . .

Lewis: Dan started the fires, and I heard the voices, but what did . . .

Michele: Falling down. Falling down. Falling down . . .

Lewis: She was a cruel friend. She played with guns and shot soup cans. But the reason I really hated her was because she always made fun of me.

Michele: London Bridge is . . .

Lewis: I know who you are!

Michele: Falling down . . .

Lewis: I never liked your fuckin' song!

Michele: Falling down . . .

Lewis: Why do you always have to sing it?

Michele: Falling down . . .

Lewis: Why do you still sing it?

Michele: Lewis, you love me. You know why I sing it. The memory of your fort remains alive in the song. You know it. Come on, sing with me. London Bridge is falling down. Falling down. Falling down. London Bridge is . . .

Lewis: I don't understand. I never knew the words to that song. I hated that song. Why would I want to sing it?

Michele: The song tells the history of your fort.

Lewis: Michele!

Michele: What?

Lewis: What happened to my fort?

Michele: Excuse me. Don't you mean *our* fort? The fort that Dan, yourself, and myself built to hide from the rest of the world.

At this moment, the lights are dimmed on stage right and simultaneously turned up on stage left. Abe lets loose an explosive scream. This breaks the deadly silence between Abe, Rita, and Damon.

Abe: Of course! He has been living in the fort the entire time. The only people in his head are those that know about it or those that can penetrate its fortress. The first is the fortress to his imaginary world.

Rita: What?

Damon: Did you try to tell us something, Abe?

Abe: Shh! This is important!

At this moment, the lights are dimmed on stage left and raised on stage right. Lewis and Michele pick up their conversation right where they left off.

Lewis: Was that why we built it?

Michele: Don't you remember? All the other kids made fun of you because you were always talking to yourself.

Lewis: I remember.

Michele: All the girls made fun of Dan because he was ugly, and he would just stare at the matches whenever he could . . .

Lewis: What did they make fun of you about?

Michele: Doesn't matter . . .

Lewis: What did they make fun of you over?

Michele: I said, it doesn't matter!

Lewis: What did they make fun of you about?

Michele: That you were my brother, and that Dan was a close friend . . . But it doesn't matter . . . What matters is that I was the normal one. I knew your fort was going to be destroyed. I didn't want them to have the pleasure of destroying it. I loved you. So I didn't allow that to happen . . .

Lewis: What do you mean? Destroying it? The fort is still there, isn't it? I was there a week or two ago with Dan.

Once again, the lights are momentarily dimmed on stage right and raised on stage left.

Abe: Of course! The fort was never destroyed in his mind! It still exists! It has only vanished! We can still save him! All we have to do is find the fort! A stupid fuckin' fort is what's keeping Lewis from experiencing the real world!

Rita: You have Damon and myself . . .

Abe: Shut up! I'll explain later!

The lights are dimmed on stage left and raised on stage right.

Michele: No, you weren't . . .

Lewis: The fort can't be destroyed. I'd go back if I only had a map. Why did I have to lose that map? If only I hadn't gone there a couple of weeks ago. Then I would have the map . . .

Michele: But you weren't there a week or two ago.

Lewis: What do you mean?

Michele: You couldn't have been there a week or two ago with Dan because . . . because Dan is dead.

Lewis: Dan's dead?

Michele: He died when somebody burned him.

Lewis: Dan got burned?

Michele: They found his body staked to a burning barrel down by the river.

Lewis: How could Dan die by fire? He loved fire. He knew all about it. Unless . . . unless I was the one that burned him. But I don't remember a river . . . What river?

Michele: The river that travels through town. You know this one. It has a creek and a small bridge that only pedestrians and bikers can pass over. You used to take me there in the fall. We would look at the colors on the trees. They changed colors all the time, especially in the fall. Remember, that's why you painted the fort orange and red.

The lights are dimmed on stage right and raised on stage left. Abe has moved closer to the mirror so that Lewis appears to be his reflection. Damon and Rita have stopped watching Lewis in order to pay closer attention to Abe.

Abe: Just like you, Lewis. As long as you can change your colors, no one can find you. That makes you free and makes it impossible for anyone to find the fort. Therefore, it can never be destroyed, and Sara can remain alive. I knew she was the reason, but I never understood why you wouldn't let me talk to her. Now I know . . . She is the princess of your fort, and you will do anything to protect her. You will never abandon her, even if it means you to have to fight a forty-year war against the rest of the world.

The lights are dimmed on stage left and raised on stage right.

Lewis: No . . . I don't . . . I painted it orange and red because . . .

Michele: The water was pretty to watch. It trickled past the rocks, changing from blue to white all the time. It could never move the rocks, remember?

The lights are dimmed on stage right and raised on stage left.

Abe: Of course! Nothing can move the rocks. They are there to stay for eternity. One has to live around them, on top of them, or underneath them. There is no way to live exactly where the rocks stand, because they don't move.

The lights are dimmed on stage left and raised on stage right.

Lewis: I can't remember.

Michele: You and Dan went there a lot also. You called it the secret burning place because you guys lit fires near the bottom of it. You would watch the fires and tell stories.

The lights are dimmed on stage right and raised on stage left.

Abe: Stories that we never gave up and stories that will never go away. They will never leave us alone.

The lights are dimmed on stage left and raised on stage right.

Lewis: How did Dan die?

Michele: I told you that he was burned.

Lewis: Who burned him?

Michele: That's a dumb question! Who do you think burned him?

Lewis: Dan?

Michele: No. Dan never lit a fire in his life. That was a lie that Mom started so that people would believe that you weren't the cause behind those fires. Besides, do you really think that Dan would burn himself?

The lights are dimmed on stage right and raised on stage left.

Abe: Mom did something nice. That doesn't fit. Why would Mom do something nice for me? She never cared. She never showed any love. She was just like Dad, and that's why I'm like this.

The lights are dimmed on stage left and raised on stage right.

Lewis: Was I? . . .

Michele: No . . .

Lewis: Then who was . . . who was the person that tried to ruin my life and Dan's, too?

Michele: What do you mean tried? They did ruin your lives.

Lewis: Who is 'they'?

Michele: Mom and Dad.

Lewis: What?

Michele: Dad burned Dan down by the river. Mom burned the church.

Lewis: But I thought both of them were dead when all that happened? I thought they burned to death in the house when I escaped?

Michele: That's what they wanted people to believe. It was easier that way. They were able to get rid of you and the voices by faking their own deaths. They hated you, and they knew that the only way out was to make it look like your fault or Dan's fault.

Lewis: What did the town think about Dan's death?

Michele: They kept it quiet. You know, out of the papers. They simply said that a youth died by the river of unknown causes. The autopsy came up with no exact cause of death, even though there were many burns found all over Dan's body.

The lights are dimmed on stage right and raised on stage left.

Abe: He can't be dead! Dan can't be dead!

The lights are dimmed on stage left and raised on stage right.

Lewis: Did he have burns on his body?

Michele: I saw them take his body away. He was broiled like a piece of hamburger meat. All of his skin had been burned, and his bones were black. It appeared as though someone had tied him to a barrel, doused him and it with gasoline, and then lit it with a match. They must have watched him burn for pure pleasure.

Lewis: I don't understand. If Mom and Dad were responsible, were you and the others meant to go along with them, or did you really die?

Michele: I escaped. I was fortunate. I saw them one night after all the kids had gone to bed. They were setting out the gas cans. The rags that were used as torches were also being prepared. They hid them outside behind a bush and went to bed. The following day, Dad came home from work early. You were supposed to be there, but you hadn't come back yet. The rest of us were watching television.

Lewis: Where was I?

The lights are dimmed on stage right and raised on stage left.

Abe: I was playing with Dan. I was at the park. I was at the fort. No one could hurt me there. Why didn't I stay there?

The lights are dimmed on stage left and raised on stage right.

Michele: You were at the park with Dan. Anyway, I was curious. Something didn't seem right, so I kept sneaking a peek in the kitchen. Mom and Dad were constantly arguing. She appeared to be having second thoughts or wanting to wait for some reason. Dad wanted to do it right away.

Lewis: Why didn't you say something?

Michele: It would have only prolonged the inevitable. After a few hours, they seemed to disappear. I left Sara and Christian watching television and walked back out. I was going to get rid of the gasoline. As I was walking out, I heard this nagging voice, but no one was there. I guess it was my conscious or subconscious trying to tell me something. So I paused for a moment . . .

Lewis: What happened?

Michele: Nothing. So I decided to head back for the house. But as I turned around, the house was suddenly covered in flames. It was almost as if the ground just burned upwards onto the side of the house. The fire raced systematically, attacking the walls, floors, and family members inside.

The lights are dimmed on stage right and raised on stage left.

Abe: The fire was so hot. I just wanted to get away. It wasn't that I didn't love the people inside or that I didn't want to protect and save them. It was just that I couldn't do it. It was not physically possible. But I could save Oscar. All I had to do was use my mind. That's why I didn't understand when they told me he died a couple of weeks later.

The lights are dimmed on stage left and raised on stage right.

Lewis: Did you see me?

Michele: I saw you racing around the side of the house. I wanted to stop you, but I couldn't.

Lewis: Why couldn't you stop me?

Michele: At the same time I saw you, I also saw Mom and Dad running away. If I said anything, they would have known that I wasn't inside. And I didn't want to take that chance.

Lewis: But how did they plan on getting away with it if they knew I wasn't going to be inside when they lit the house on fire?

Michele: Apparently, they had been planning on saying that it was kids playing with matches, but you weren't there, so they couldn't say that. No one would believe them.

Lewis: So what happened to them?

Michele: Apparently, they fled. After I saw them leave, I tried to get your attention. But it was too late. You ran inside the burning house because you wanted to save Oscar. When they brought you out, you were in shock and never came out of it. I was left alone. I watched as the police tried to talk to you. You started to go insane. You were jumping personalities. It took the police a week and a half to get a real name from you. Everyone in the house was considered dead, but you.

Lewis: If I was in police custody, why did everyone think I started the other fires?

Michele: You were staying at Grandma's under a police guard. And no one could account for where you were at the time of the fires. As time went on and the police couldn't find any suspects, they simply said that you were the one that started the house on fire. They said that your insanity or shock or whatever it was, was just an act. I wanted to help you, but if I did, I had to worry about Mom and Dad finding me.

Lewis: Where did they go?

Michele: Apparently, they set up camp by the river.

Lewis: So what happens now?

Michele: Well, you have to leave the darkness.

Lewis: I like it here.

Michele: If you leave the darkness, you will be able to meet me.

Lewis: I would like that.

Michele: I will save your name, and Mom and Dad will be looked for more intensely.

Lewis: Mom and Dad are being looked for?

Michele: As we speak. But I need you to come out of this state before I can do anything more. If you don't, I have no living eye witnesses.

Lewis: What about yourself?

Michele: I won't become a witness unless you become one.

Lewis: So I have to be sane again?

Michele: Yes.

Lewis: How long has it been?

Michele: A long time.

Lewis: How long is 'a long time'?

Michele: I'm not sure anymore. I stopped counting the years. Let's just say you aren't a young man anymore. Don't let them waste any more of your life. Help me catch them.

The lights are raised on the entire stage so that the audience can see that Rita and Damon are staring at Abe the same way Michele is staring at Lewis. After a few moments, the lights are dimmed, and the curtains are closed.

SCENE II

Setting:

The stage is once again split into two sides. On the stage right, Lewis Strange is sitting alone at a table. Abe is found standing behind him. He has just finished cleaning a mess that was left from Lewis's lunch. Rita is also in the room. She is standing to Lewis's left near the side wall by the mirror.

Through the mirror behind Rita, the audience can see Damon, Michele, Bill Strange, Hillary Strange, and two police officers huddled in Abe's office. Each appears anxious to listen to the conversation for different reasons.

Abe: When did this happen, Lewis?

Lewis: I can't remember.

Abe: How did it make you feel?

Lewis: It made me feel like I was trash.

Abe: But you aren't trash!

Lewis: How do you know?

Abe: Because you're human.

Lewis: No, I'm not!

Abe: You are! You have a soul and a mind! You just haven't directed it in the right way yet! Someday you will.

Lewis: But I can't remember what I do! I'm abnormal because I can't find the light!

Abe: Lewis, will you let me help you?

Lewis: I'm not sure . . .

Abe: Will you let me lead you out of the darkness?

Lewis: Where will I go when you lead me out?

Abe: You know as well as I that you can't go back to the light. Therefore, I will lead you beyond the light to a great place.

Lewis: I don't want to go there!

Abe: I can bring you reality.

Lewis: I don't want reality!

At this moment, Rita breaks her silence and begins to speak. A look of disgust flashes across Abe's face, but it is too late. Rita has gained Lewis's attention, and she moves toward him as she responds to him.

Rita: But reality wants you!

Lewis: What?

Rita: Reality wants you!

Lewis: Who said that?

Rita: Turn around, Lewis.

Lewis: Why?

Rita: Because reality wants you.

Lewis: Who are you?

Rita: I am reality, and I have come to claim you, since you won't allow Abe to do it.

Lewis: I hate reality! It only tries to hurt me!

Rita: No, it doesn't. Reality is trying to save you.

Lewis: Save me from what?

Rita: Yourself.

Lewis: I don't need to be saved. I'm perfectly all right by myself. All I need is for these voices to leave me alone.

Rita: But that is the purpose of reality. It will destroy the voices.

Lewis: No, it won't!

Rita: What will reality do then?

Lewis: Reality will destroy me! Reality created the voices! Reality destroyed the bodies that belonged to the voices! Reality has left those voices with me!

Rita: No, it was your imagination that left you with the voices. We want to take them away. Follow me, Lewis.

Lewis: I'm not sure . . .

Rita: Just give me a chance. Will you give me a chance?

Lewis: I suppose.

Rita: Abe is your friend?

Lewis: Yes.

Rita: Abraham is a part of reality?

Lewis: Yes.

Rita: Then reality owns one friend?

Lewis: Yes.

Rita: The therapist across from you is your friend?

Lewis: Yes.

Rita: He is also from reality?

Lewis: Yes.

Rita: Therefore, reality owns two friends.

Lewis: Yes.

Rita: How many does imagination allow?

As this question is raised, Lewis appears to become distracted. He stops looking in the general direction of Rita and begins to stare directly at the audience. The audience receives the impression that Lewis has forgotten about everything occurring around him and now is privately speaking to the audience as if its identity were that of Lewis's sister, Sara Strange.

Lewis: Not now, I'm busy . . . No, I'm busy with this woman. She's trying to get rid of you. I can't let that happen . . . Shut up! I'm talking to someone!

While Lewis is speaking, the audience is also able to see Abe nod as if he understands exactly why Lewis has switched conversations. When Lewis completes his thought, Abe responds by blurting out his reaction to Lewis's comments.

Abe: So that's the problem? If you leave the world of the voices, you will lose your sister forever. You already lost her once and don't want to lose her again.

Lewis: No, it isn't!

Abe: Lewis . . .

Lewis: Why are you always attempting to be a psychiatrist?

Abe: Because I am.

Lewis: You are not Abraham.

Abe: You're right. I don't sit on a throne in Washington D.C. I sit in a chair in a room at St. John's Asylum for the mentally challenged, with you. We sit together in Seattle. Although that normally allows me to escape to Washington . . .

Lewis: I wish I could escape . . . escape this world with all these . . .

Abe: With what? . . . With the voices?

Lewis: I want to escape.

Abe: You can. It isn't that difficult. All you have to do is listen to Rita and myself. Then you will come back to reality. You will kill the voices and the pain they cause you.

Once again, at this moment, Lewis appears to become distant from those that are seated near him. Again, he is staring directly at the audience, and this time the audience receives the impression that Lewis thinks it his old friend, Dan.

Lewis: I don't want to burn them! They make sense. They speak logically. They are my friends! But . . . but I never . . . I don't want to burn things anymore! No . . .

Lewis's statement is cut off as Michele begins to speak on stage left.

Michele: My God! Lewis thinks he is talking to Dan. Why couldn't I just let things develop as they should? Why did I have to push him to complete that plan? Why did I have to revive all those ugly childhood memories? He had forgotten them for so long . . . We were living a new life, separate from all that was and all that ever could be. And then I . . . with my stupid plotting scheme to get money . . . Why was I so greedy?

With these words, Michele races out of the room and into the room that already holds Abe, Rita, and Lewis. Meanwhile, on stage right, Rita makes an attempt at bringing Lewis back to herself and Abe.

Rita: Reality will not go away. You will always be able to find us, but soon we will not stay around so you can talk to us anytime you want. Abe and I will leave.

Michele swings the droop open and enters, immediately blurting out a phrase she already knows the answer to.

Michele: Did he talk yet?

Lewis: Who's that?

Abe: It's Michele. She wants you back, too. She loves you. She's part of your family, and she misses you.

Lewis: Yeah, but she's not Sara. She never loved me or Sara. She just wants to see Mom and Dad in jail.

Michele: Lewis! That's not true! I have always loved you. I will always love you. You are my brother. Come on! Listen to them! Come back to reality!

Lewis: I can live with my sister. I won't need you! I won't need an audience!

Michele: Yes! You can live with me!

Rita: Yes! You can live with her!

Lewis: Shut up, Jilie! I'm not a killer; I have never killed before! I know I'm right, because they told me so! The people from reality told me! I know I am right, because you died in the fire! I never liked the way you cleaned our house anyway!

Rita appears confused by Lewis's comments. She looks to Abe and Michele to see if they are confused. Michele holds an expression of confusion, yet Abe appears to understand exactly what is occurring.

Rita: What's happening?

Abe: Talk to us, Lewis.

Lewis: Mom and Dad want me to explain that Michele didn't do what she says they did.

Michele: I can help on this one.

Michele turns and heads to the door. She opens it and says a few words into the hallway that no one in the room can understand. After a few seconds, she reenters the room with a couple of police officers. Between them, an elderly couple is walking. They are in handcuffs. Meanwhile, within the room, Abe is completely immune to the events that are transpiring. However, Rita's surprise and fear can genuinely be seen in her face.

Michele: Here are Mom and Dad. They have been brought in for questioning. I just couldn't wait for you anymore. I didn't want them to get away with what they did to me and you.

The old man is the first to speak out of the handcuffed couple. However, his statements are quickly followed by that of the elderly woman.

Bill: I'm not sorry!

Hillary: We didn't do anything!

Bill: It was that vagrant!

Hillary: We aren't his parents!

Bill: You can't prove we are!

Michele: But I can! Lewis, I traced their records. I have a match. This is Mom and Dad. I got them! Now, let's make them pay!

Rita: Make them pay, Lewis!

On the other side of the stage, Damon sits alone in Abe's office. He has watched the whole scene through the two-way mirror.

Damon: How can these people all be so stupid? They're playing out a charade that will never work. They speak of reality, but they only feed the imagination. Lewis's true secret will never come out in this fashion. His riddles will remain unsolved for eternity, unless I tell their answers . . . but I could never do that. He has played the game much too well, and as for the rest of them . . . Abe is going to lose. He just doesn't understand the magnitude of the problem. Rita, she has won her initial battles, but her problem is that she believes what she has created. And Michele . . . Michele is too naïve to play this game. She is only a pawn for Lewis to confuse Abe and Rita. I must go into that room and watch this game play out.

There is a three-to-four second silence here while all the comments above are left to linger on the stage. The short period of silence is broken as Damon enters through the door from the hallway. He quickly moves to the back of the stage and stands behind Rita. A smile stretches across his face as he waits for events to unfold.

Lewis: Let's make them pay!

Lewis's voice sounds vindictive, but before continuing with his thought, he switches again to another random topic.

Lewis: What about my doctors? Can they come, too?

Rita: We're here.

Lewis: No! I mean Clare and Damon.

Rita signals behind her to Damon for him to move forward. He follows her hand gestures and approaches the table so that he is standing next to Rita.

Rita: Lewis, read that for me.

Lewis: It says Damon.

Rita: That's right. You spent so much time with him that you made into part of your mind. Especially after that one time you attacked him. In order to save himself, he had to beat you up pretty bad.

Damon: Sorry about that.

Lewis: What about Clare?

Abe: We don't know where you got her from.

Rita: Hopefully, someday you will be able to tell us. You're sane. Tell me your name.

Lewis: My name is Lewis Strange.

Damon: She's right. You are sane.

Abe: Lewis, are you there? We can't afford to lose you. Otherwise, they might lock you up forever.

Michele: I want these two put in jail!

Abe: What is your name?

Lewis: My name is Lewis Strange. . . Shut up!

Abe: Dammit! Everyone out!

The lights are shut off, and the curtains close.

Schizophrenic Statue

Dan Adams

Ten|16
PRESS
www.ten16press.com - Waukesha, WI

To my parents, whom I owe my greatest gratitude in the pursuit of my writing career. Thank you for always understanding the voices in my head.

Schizophrenic Statue

Dan Adams

CAST OF CHARACTERS

(accents in parentheses)

The Family:
Reverend Bill (Irish)
Christian (Old South American)
Hillary (Irish)
Lewis (Midwest American)
Michele (Texan American)
Oscar
Sara (Irish)

The Therapists:
Abe (Scottish)
Chuck (London)
Clare (French)
Damon (German)
Ludwig Beeto (Swedish)
Rita Flemming (French)

The Rest of the Cast:
Dan Adams (Midwest American)
Abe Lincoln
Allistair (Italian)
Dan (Midwest American)
Emma Kenda (Texan)
Jilie (Irish)
Owen (Boston)
President Ford (Washington, D.C.)

Dan Adams: My name is Lewis Strange...

SCENE 1

Setting:

The stage is very dark, therefore making it very difficult for the audience to see. However, through the darkness, the audience should be able to see a room. The room has a window, but the shade is drawn on that window so that no outside light can enter the room.

A spotlight breaks through this darkness and is focused on Lewis Strange. He is sitting at a table with three chairs. Lewis's chair is facing opposite the darkest side of the room. A second chair is facing the audience. Meanwhile, the third chair is facing the only window in the room, directly behind Lewis Strange.

The back of the room contains a large glass mirror. When light is present, Lewis's image can be seen in the mirror. His physique is tall and skinny. The remnants of what once were braces can be seen near his teeth. These facts are revealed to the audience when the spotlight is focused on Lewis Strange.

The floor of the room is black. The walls are grayish in color but appear to have been white a long time ago. The table is long and square. It resembles a table that one might see in any high school cafeteria. There is nothing on top of it.

7

Beyond the room, there is an elevated step. A statue of Abraham Lincoln sits silently. During the scene, a spotlight is focused on Abraham Lincoln so that the audience is reminded of his constant presence.

The motion of the characters throughout the scene is nonstop. Characters will enter the stage and speak to Lewis. If a character enters from stage right, the next character is to enter from stage left. As soon as Lewis switches his attention to the next character, the first exits the stage the way he/she entered. This is a continual process so that the audience is left with the impression that Lewis is never alone.

Lewis: Shut up!

Clare: Someday somebody will understand. You know it takes time . . . It takes time for people to understand those who are different.

Lewis: How am I different?

Jilie: It doesn't matter! You're a killer! It was your fault. It shouldn't have happened, but you made it happen. You should be ashamed.

Rita: Don't listen to her! She's wrong! You did everything you could! It wasn't your fault! You tried! You really tried!

Lewis: Did I? I can't remember . . . I see it clearly sometimes, but then . . . Then again, those red people down there won't let me. They say I had no part of it. I'm so confused . . .

Bill: But why? The Bible says, "Thou shalt not kill." What is so hard to understand? You broke that commandment. You let the town, your family, and me down . . . Not to mention yourself. God didn't create the Commandments to be broken.

Lewis: Did I break that commandment? I don't think I did . . .

Ford: Oh yes, you did. You are evil! You belong in that place! That horrible place where all the people like you go! I only wish I could lock everyone up like we did with you! Someday, everybody like you will live in those places permanently!

Lewis: No! He said I didn't belong! He said I never did it! He said you were wrong and that it was all a mistake . . . a giant confusion of reality . . . a misunderstanding. He told me I'd be all right if . . .

Christian: Are you all right? How do you know if you are? You still listen to us. You never act on your own. What is it that convinces you that you are all right?

Lewis: I don't know. I guess . . . I guess I took his word, but now . . . now I'm not so sure . . .

Hillary: You are crazy! You were crazy once, and that makes you crazy forever! I hate you! I wish you weren't mine. I wish I would have aborted you. Then you would know . . . you would know how wrong you are!

Lewis: No! Don't say that! I . . . I loved you! I still do love . . .

Allistar: You are nothing! Your life amounts to nothing, and you've always been nothing! You are a worthless excuse for a human being!

Lewis: Don't say that! Oscar survived. Doesn't that account for something?

Sara: No! Oscar was worthless! Why couldn't you save Michele or me?

Lewis: Because there was no time . . . Was there?

Dan: Let's kill them all! Come on, it won't be that hard. You like fire. All you have to do is light that match again. It was so easy the last time. It was pretty, too, or didn't you think it was?

Lewis: But I didn't do it! I was away! It wasn't my fault! Oscar didn't die until weeks later.

Ludwig: Yes, but animals don't go to heaven, do they? Whose fault is it that your beloved family is gone?

Lewis: Clare said it wasn't my fault . . .

Damon: Clare is not your therapist!

Lewis: Why won't all these snakes just leave me alone?

Chuck: I don't see any snakes. I just see Abraham.

Lewis: Abe helped me. He helped me to remember my childhood.

Michele: London Bridge is falling down . . .

Lewis: Michele, is that . . .

Abe: Don't listen to them! Listen to me!

Bill: Thou shalt not kill!

Hillary: You are crazy!

Abe: You are sane!

Rita: It wasn't your fault!

Ford: Let's lock all you crazy people away!

Dan: You are an arsonist! You like fire!

Clare: Someday, somebody will understand you.

Michele: London Bridge is falling down . . .

Damon: Clare is not your therapist!

Chuck: I don't see any snakes.

Allistar: Your life is nothing. You are nothing.

Sara: Do you want to play?

Owen: You deserved to die!

Jilie: You didn't try to save your family, did you?

Christian: Isn't this worse than death?

SCENE 2

Setting:

Lewis Strange is sitting at the table as he was in Scene 1. However, on the wall opposite Lewis, the audience is able to see the pond that is found in front of the Washington Monument. The water is not frozen, and snow can be seen on the surrounding landscape. Again, a spotlight is focused on the statue of Abraham Lincoln that rests behind the room. Throughout the scene, the lights become increasingly stronger in order to imitate the rising of the sun.

Lewis: I said, be quiet! Leave me alone! All I want to be is alone, alone with Abe . . . Abe understands me. He understands that I just want to be free. Why won't they let me go free? I've done what they told me, but they still follow me and haunt me. You built this land, these people, on freedom and liberty. Why don't those regulations apply to everyone? Why do they restrict people like me and make me unhealthy?

Jilie: It's because you let your family die! Christian, Michele, Sara, Bill, and Hillary . . . They all died, and it was all your fault!

Lewis: Jilie, don't say that! I didn't do it. I could do nothing but watch. I only had a moment and the . . . the house was so hot. There was so much smoke in the air . . . I couldn't breathe. Especially after spending the entire day in the park. I grabbed what I could . . . what I could find and ran. I was only a child. I was so afraid. I mean, if I got out, shouldn't they have been able to get out on their own?

Jilie: You could have attempted to save them instead of saving Oscar. It was worthless to save him. After all, you knew he would be a burden to you.

Lewis: But, I loved Oscar. He was always there for me.

Jilie: So, you loved a pet more than your family?

Lewis: No! That isn't true! Oscar was by the door. Oscar was the easiest to free. I didn't know where anyone else was. But Oscar . . . Oscar was reliable. He was always in the same spot, and he was always there when I needed him. I had to save him! I couldn't let him die! It would have been wrong!

Jilie: So it was right to let your family die?

Lewis: No, but . . .

Jilie: But nothing. That damn animal was the reason you let your family die! Where is he now? Dead! That's right! You also let him die! You just waited a few weeks to kill him! You wanted everyone around you to die! You just waited with Oscar because you knew he would be easier to kill in the long run!

Lewis: That's not true. I loved Oscar! I didn't kill him on purpose. I just didn't have the money to feed him. Oscar was the closest to the door. He was the easiest to save.

Jilie: No! Christian was in the room just around the corner! Sara was in the room at the top of the stairs! What stopped you from saving them? You wanted them dead! Congratulations, they are dead and so is Oscar. Now you have their voices just as you have mine. I hope they haunt you forever!

The lights fade.

SCENE 3

Setting:

When the lights are raised, Lewis Strange can be seen sitting inside a confession box similar to the kind one would find in a Catholic church. The confession box has taken the spot where the table rested in the previous scene.

The side of the box that the Pastor is normally on is missing. In its place, Lewis can see the same wall that he previously saw an image of Washington D.C. on.

However, the wall that formerly displayed a portion of Washington, D.C. now displays a steeple of a church. The steeple of the church is beautiful, but the rest of the church is absent. At the top of the steeple, Lewis can see a man. He is dressed in a pastor's clothes and appears to be hovering above the steeple.

Bill: How old are you, son?

Lewis: Nine . . . Wait! . . . I mean eighteen . . . I'm not sure. What year is this?

Bill: 1994.

Lewis: But I thought it was 1988. I was going home for dinner. Mom said if I came home from the park in time, I could eat dinner with Christian and Sara. Mom said I wouldn't have to worry because Dad would be at work . . . Where am I?

Bill: You are here.

Lewis: Where is here, exactly?

Bill: In a moment, but first, tell me why you would worry about your dad being at dinner? (*No answer.*) Why did you fear your dad at dinner, Lewis?

Lewis: I can't tell you, Father. I mean, you are a priest, but I can't tell you.

Bill: Why can't you tell me? After all, I am your father. I am your priest.

Lewis: That's exactly why!

Bill: Lewis, you are not making any sense. Now, tell me why you could not eat dinner with your father, otherwise, I will be forced to use the rod.

Lewis: Because dad was mean! Dad made sure things went wrong. He always had a stick of some sort and . . . and he seemed to enjoy using it.

Bill: Your dad never hit you, did he? (*No answer.*) Lewis, you are talking nonsense and blasphemy, aren't you?

Lewis: No! I am not talking nonsense!

Bill: I think we ought to use the rod on you, because you are lying!

Lewis: I am not lying!

Bill: In the Bible, the Commandments tell us, "Thou shalt not lie."

Lewis: I'm not lying! Dad hit me! He did it because he enjoyed it! He enjoyed hurting me!

Bill: Your dad loved you and was following what the Bible told him to do. "Spare the rod and spoil the child." He didn't want you to be spoiled, so he used the rod more often than most parents. He didn't want you to do the wrong things later on in life. I would have done the same, myself.

Lewis: But you did . . . I mean . . . You are the same. You have done the same. The priest, Mom, and Dad were all evil. They told me things that weren't true so that they could punish me more.

Bill: You aren't religious, are you? (*No answer.*) I reckon I could know. I am your father. You never came to church. That's why I had to hit you so much.

Lewis: And that's why I burned you!

Bill: So you admit that you did start the fire?

Lewis: No, I don't think I did . . . I can't remember . . .

Bill: But then, why did you say you burned me?

Lewis: I don't know. It felt right. It was what was on my mind. Abe told me to say it.

Bill: But the Bible says, "Thou shalt not kill." To think of killing is as bad as the action itself. You should never think of physically harming another person, but you did. You thought of killing your father, and then you did it! You lit his home on fire! Then you became even more of a heathen by going to his place of work: the father's house.

Lewis: What do you mean?

Bill: The Bible tells us . . .

Lewis: Remember, I don't go to church! I don't believe in God! I don't follow those Commandments, because you teach them! Maybe someday, I'll find a father who cares! And then I will follow those Commandments!

Bill: That isn't very religious . . .

Lewis: I follow no religion! Jilie follows no religion! Oscar follows no religion! . . .

Clare: That was a mistake.

The lights fade. In the darkness, the confession box is lifted, and the table is placed back in its original position.

SCENE 4

Setting:

When the lights come back up, Lewis Strange is seen sitting at the table across from Rita Flemming. Her dusty colored hair sharply contrasts her white sport coat. The tag on her sweater reads Rita, but Lewis always identifies her as Clare. Rita's eyes are reddish in color. Rita holds a small notebook pad in front of her in which she periodically records information that Lewis tells her.

Clare: Now, let's start again. I want to know your name.

Lewis: Lewis Strange.

Clare: When were you born?

Lewis: A long time ago.

Clare: How old are you?

Lewis: I am nineteen.

Clare: How can you be nineteen if you were born eight years ago?

Lewis: Wait . . . I was born nineteen years ago! Now, I remember it clearly. But what happened to the past eleven years? Where have I been for that period of time?

Clare: Let's start again. What is your name?

Lewis: Jilie.

Clare: I thought you were Lewis?

Lewis: No, I didn't!

Clare: I see . . . Where are you from?

Lewis: I don't know. Where do you want me to be from?

Clare: When were you born?

Lewis: That's easy, but I can't tell you.

Clare: Why? (*No answer.*) Why can't you tell me?

Lewis: Because then Lewis will know.

Clare: What will Lewis know?

Lewis: That my name is Dan.

Clare: Dan, please let me talk to Jilie.

Lewis: Jilie got tired of this game. She went to play with Dan.

Clare: I thought you said your name was Dan?

Lewis: I was Dan, a long time ago. I'm hungry. I want to eat.

Dan: You can't eat!

Smoke flows across the stage, and the audience is able to see a church burning on the side wall of the room. When the fire burns out on its own, the image of the church fades. During this moment, Clare has exited stage right, and Dan has entered stage left. The audience is now able to see Dan sitting where Clare originally was seated.

Lewis: I have to go home for dinner and get some food. Then I can play. Then we can go to the park and shoot my BB guns at those squirrels.

Dan: You can't go home!

Lewis: Why can't I go home? My mom said to be home by four so that I can eat and leave before dad gets home from church.

Dan: Your dad has already been home. Now, he is home eternally.

Lewis: How do you know? (*No answer.*) You've been with me all day. If you know that my dad came home early, I should know . . . Shouldn't I?

Dan: Let's just say that Reverend Strange was a little closer to the fire of hell than he expected to be at this junction in his life.

Lewis: What do you mean?

Dan: You know how much I hate to see you cry when he beats you before you come play with me, so I took care of the problem. I'm just sorry that Christian and Sara had to be there. I liked them.

Lewis: What are you talking about, Dan?

Dan: Remember the first time, the first time he beat you. Whose fault was it?

The stage falls to darkness. During this period, the room is changed to Lewis's living room as a child. He is seated on a couch, and his father is staring into his eyes. Dan is seated in a chair off to the side. Lewis has just been caught playing with matches because Dan encouraged him to.

Bill: Son, were you playing with matches?

Lewis: Dad . . .

Bill: I told you never to play with matches! You could have burned the entire house down!

Lewis: Dad, I wasn't . . .

With the end of those words, Bill gives Lewis a beating while the lights fade. Moments later, when the lights are raised, Lewis finds himself sitting across from Clare, with Dan at his left.

Clare: Are you all right?

Lewis: Are you all right?

Dan: Are you all right?

Lewis: I need to go home and eat. I will be back here at four to play in the park.

Dan: No! You won't! You will be at the precinct all night! Just don't let them know it was me! I did it for you! Don't rat on me!

Lewis: What do you mean?

Dan: You know what I did! Stop pretending that you don't know just because your therapist friend is here! After all, you thought of it! I know all your thoughts, because I live out what you think. It was so easy. All I did was strike a match to that can of gasoline and . . .

Lewis: You didn't. I only thought it would be neat to see my house in flames. I never really wanted to do it! I really didn't want . . .

Dan: Is that why you had the gasoline and matches hidden in your room? I knew you wanted it done. But I also knew that you would never go through with it, so I burned them for you, all of them! Yet, I do have to give you some credit. After all, you did get all the materials for me. Guess that makes us even. I won't even charge you a favor for . . .

Lewis: I had the materials, but I never wanted . . .

Dan: Yes, you did! Otherwise, I would not have done it.

The lights fade. After a few moments, the lights are raised, and Lewis finds himself staring at an image of the Washington landscape near the Lincoln Memorial. A large splash is heard. On the wall, the audience and Lewis are able to see an image of his pet dog, Oscar, swimming peacefully across the Memorial Pool. In the background, the statue of Abraham Lincoln can be seen by the audience. The lights dim once again, and the curtains close.

SCENE 5

Setting:

Lewis Strange is sitting at the table as in Scene 1. Five years have passed since the beginning of the play. Lewis is now a much older man. His face holds the weight of a large, black beard. It needs to be combed or shaven, as does his hair. His eyes are very glossy and distant. The metallic braces have been removed from his teeth.

Lewis is sitting across from a therapist by the name of Damon. He is a short, skinny man who wears glasses. Throughout the scene, Damon can be seen wiping them clean with a white handkerchief that he keeps with his pens in the right front pocket of his overcoat. Damon is wearing a long, white overcoat with his name embroidered on the right side near the heart.

Damon is accompanied by two men. Each of these men appear to be three-hundred pounds in weight, holding no fat on their toned frames. Both men have name tags, but Lewis is unable to make out what the tags say.

Damon: Lewis! . . . Are you there? Lewis! You are there, aren't you? . . . Lewis! . . . Where are you? (*Lewis remains silent.*)

Damon: Lewis! Listen to me! I am your therapist . . . I am your friend. Please, if you can hear me, give me a sign so that I know to stay. Otherwise, I will be forced to leave and see my other patients. (*Lewis's eyes open and shut numerous times.*)

Damon: What's your name? (*Lewis now closes his eyes.*)

Damon: I want to know your name . . . (*Damon is cut off when Lewis spits in his face.*)

Damon: I want to know your name immediately, or I will be forced to allow these two men to restrain you again!

Lewis: Fuck off! . . . I want to speak to Clare.

Damon: Who is Clare?

Lewis: Clare is my therapist.

Damon: No, I am your therapist.

Lewis: I want Clare!

Damon: Who is Clare? You never told me about Clare before. Was she part of your family?

Lewis: Clare is my therapist.

Damon: No! I am your therapist.

Lewis: Clare is my therapist!

Damon: Lewis, what's my name?

Lewis: Clare's my therapist!

The audience can see Lewis begin to rise from his chair. However, he is immediately forced to sit down by the two men next to Damon.

Damon: No! Rita is your therapist. I am your therapist. Clare is a friend of yours that neither of us have met, and we both would be honored if you introduced her to us.

Lewis: No! Only I can talk to my therapist.

Damon: I am your therapist! Now, what is my name?

Lewis: Clare is my therapist . . . Clare is my therapist . . . Clare is my therapist . . .

Damon: Fine! Clare can be your therapist, but then, who am I?

Lewis: You're Damon!

Damon: Good. How do you know me?

Lewis: You're my therapist.

Damon: Is it all right for me to speak with you and ask you some questions?

Lewis: You may, but whom do you want to speak with?

Damon: Can I please speak to Clare?

Lewis: No! Nobody speaks to Clare but me.

Damon: Fine. I would like to speak to Lewis. Is that okay?

Lewis: I think that can be arranged.

Damon: Who is Clare?

Lewis: A friend.

Damon: Is she a good friend?

Lewis: No. She is just a friend who understands me and always listens to me.

Damon: Does she ask you questions?

Lewis: Yes.

Damon: What kind of questions?

Lewis: What my name is, where I come from, what I do. You know, the standard, boring stuff. Nothing of interest.

Damon: Can I ask you some of that boring information?

Lewis: I suppose.

Damon: What is your name?

Lewis: Dan.

Damon: What do you do?

Lewis: I burn things.

Damon: Why?

Lewis: Because Jilie tells us to.

Damon: Who's Jilie?

Lewis: I am Jilie.

Damon: I thought you said you were Dan?

Lewis: No. Dan's dead . . .

Damon: How did Dan die?

Lewis: He burned to death at a church.

Damon: What was he doing at a church?

Lewis: Confessing.

Damon: What was he confessing?

Lewis: Attempting to murder Oscar.

Damon: Anything else?

Lewis: No.

Damon: You sure?

Lewis: Yes! Why?

Damon: Because, in the past, you told me that he was confessing to murdering your family.

Lewis: No. I told him that was all right. I understood why he did it. I forgave him. But the fact that he had murdered Oscar . . . that was wrong. That was the sin he had to confess.

Damon: Who's Oscar?

Lewis: Jilie will tell you.

Damon: I thought I was talking to Jilie.

Lewis: No. You were talking to Lewis.

Damon: Who am I talking to now?

Lewis: My name is Clare.

Damon: Clare, what do you do?

Lewis: I heal people.

Damon: What do you heal them from?

Lewis: Mental insanity.

Damon: How old are you?

Lewis: Thirty.

Damon: How old is Lewis?

Lewis: Forty-seven.

Damon: But he claims to be eight?

Lewis: He doesn't want to remember.

Damon: Remember what?

Lewis: His past.

Damon: What happened in his past?

Lewis: I can't tell you confidential information. You know that, Doctor.

Damon: How long did you treat him?

Lewis: Eleven years.

Damon: Then what happened?

Lewis: He appeared sane, so I let him go.

Damon: Was he sane?

Lewis: I think he might have been sane because all our conversations seemed to be games to him, but I don't know. He doesn't know. And honestly, after talking to Dan, I never want to know . . .

Damon: Who was Dan, exactly?

Lewis: You haven't met him?

Damon: We've met, but . . .

Lewis: You mean Lewis didn't introduce you properly? That ought to be changed. Dan . . .

Christian: Dan burned us to death, didn't he, Lewis?

With this voice, the stage has become dark, and a spotlight is focused on Christian as he enters stage left and walks over to the table. In the darkness, Damon has exited stage right. When Christian sits down across from Lewis, the lights are raised, and Lewis begins to speak.

Lewis: It can't be you! Dan killed you! Didn't he?

Christian: Come on, Lewis. You know you can't kill your voice of reason.

Lewis: I didn't try to! Dan did! It was all Dan!

Christian: Whatever . . .

Lewis: Really, I didn't try . . .

Christian: Yes, you did! Now, on to more important things. Are you suffering?

Lewis: Yes, it's so painful . . .

Christian: But you like pain, don't you? You gave your family a lot of pain.

Lewis: I just want them to leave me alone. I want you to leave me alone. I've had enough. I've said I'm sorry. Isn't that enough?

Christian: No, I'm sorry. That just isn't good enough.

Lewis: What more do you want?

Christian: I want you to suffer! I told you that you would suffer for killing us! You can't act unreasonably and expect everything to be all right! There are consequences for people that act as you did! Your consequence is the voices!

Lewis: Where is the rod?

Christian: Why did you do it?

Lewis: Do what . . .

Christian: You know what you did.

Lewis: What did I do?

Christian: You murdered your family!

Lewis: I did?

Christian: Yes, you did! Now, why? Why did you do it?

Lewis: I didn't do it! Dan did!

Christian: I know Dan did! That is exactly why I'm asking you! (*No answer.*) Is it not wrong to kill people?

Lewis: Yes.

Christian: Did you think about killing your family? . . . Did you think about killing your family? . . . I'm going to ask you one final time. Did you think about killing your family?

Lewis: Yes.

Christian: Did you not want your family dead?

Lewis: Yes! I wanted them to die! I wanted my family to die! . . . Are you happy? Is that what you wanted me to say? . . . Will you leave me alone now?

Christian: So who did you tell about this?

Lewis: I told Clare, Oscar, and . . .

Christian: Lewis, who else did you tell? (*No answer.*) Lewis . . .

Lewis: And Dan.

Christian: So . . . It is also reasonable to assume that you told each one a different way you wanted them to die?

Lewis: Yes.

Christian: Clare is a person you confide your secrets in, correct?

Lewis: Yes.

Christian: It takes time, but she always manages to convince you to tell her some of your secrets. Isn't that correct?

Lewis: Yes.

Christian: Clare is your psychologist?

Lewis: Yes.

Christian: Oscar is your second best friend?

Lewis: Yes.

Christian: Oscar is always there for you, isn't he?

Lewis: Yes.

Christian: What is Oscar?

Lewis: A dog.

Christian: What kind of dog?

Lewis: My pet dog.

Christian: But what kind of dog is he?

Lewis: A boxer.

Christian: No, that's not what I mean . . . Where is Oscar now?

Lewis: Next to me, in the doghouse.

Christian: Lewis, there is no doghouse beside you.

The lights are darkened. Simultaneously, in a small area on stage left, the lights are raised. In this area, the audience is able to see a room similar to the one that was just seen. Another actor will be required to play Lewis Strange, as it is impossible to make the switch without affecting the motion of the play. A group of doctors are standing around Lewis. He is staring at the wall where the Washington Monument is projected and Oscar, his pet boxer, is running through

Memorial Park. Meanwhile, Ludwig, a short Swedish man, is seen speaking with the three doctors that are present in the room: two male and one female.

Ludwig: Lewis needs help. He can't even tell that his imaginary pet, a boxer, is imaginary. He lives in a world that is completely different from any that we know. Until he can live in our world, I feel that it is best for you to stay here and work with him. I don't believe that Lewis can survive in the outside world at this moment in his life. He has had a traumatic experience, and I think it would be best if you keep him contained within these facilities at St. John's Medical Hospital for the Mentally Challenged.

Rita: I agree.

Damon: I agree.

Abe: Thank you for your help, Doctor Beeto. We appreciate the long trip you made in order to help us. Rita and I were in disagreement, and Damon is still aspiring to grow in knowledge.

Ludwig: No problem. Glad to be of help to a famous man like you, Abe, and to a young, aspiring doctor like Damon. Lewis is an interesting patient. Would you mind if I continue speaking with him?

Abe: No, go right ahead.

The lights fade once again, and when they are turned up, the four doctors have vanished. Once again, Lewis is found sitting across the table from Christian.

Christian: Do you remember that day?

Lewis: Yes.

Christian: I just wanted to make sure you remembered . . . I wanted to make sure you remembered how awful your past was and how three out of four doctors felt you were completely crazy!

Lewis: Abe didn't think I was crazy!

Christian: Not completely, but the others did, and you doubt Abe's reliance?

Lewis: No, I don't!

Christian: Then why do you only tell Clare your secrets?

Lewis: I tell Abe the same things I tell Clare.

Christian: Yes, but when you confide in Abe, the secrets are forced from you.

Lewis: Yes.

Christian: So, who do you trust?

Lewis: Clare.

Christian: No. Clare is a mirage. You don't trust her. You tell her only what she can pry away from your twisted mind. But you let her believe that it is given willingly. Why do you trust Abe and Abe alone?

Lewis: How did you know I trust Abe?

Christian: I know, and I know why you trust him.

Lewis: If you know me so well, tell me why I trust him.

Christian: You trust Abe because Abe would not admit you were crazy, and because you know who Clare really is!

Lewis: Yes, but how . . .

Christian: Let's get back to our conversation. Oscar is a dog that didn't exist in the past and doesn't exist now.

Lewis: No.

Christian: Do I have to show you the memory again? Four doctors in one room, and they all saw you show Ludwig a dog that wasn't there.

Lewis: All right! Oscar didn't exist in the past, and he doesn't exist now.

Christian: Dan is your best friend, isn't he?

Lewis: Yes.

Christian: Dan is an arsonist?

Lewis: What does arsonist mean?

Christian: An arsonist is someone who burns things for no particular reason. They burn them time and time again for the mere sight of the orange ball of flame. Dan . . .

Lewis: Dan wanted me to burn things for no particular reason. I remember when he got Dad to beat me up for the first time. He was egging me on to burn the carpet. He liked fire. Therefore, he had to be an arsonist.

Christian: Was Dan an arsonist?

Lewis: Yes, I believe he was.

Christian: Then following on your reasoning through this entire conversation, you told a psychiatrist whom you don't trust, an imaginary dog, and an arsonist that you wanted your family to die a horrible death?

Lewis: I did.

Christian: Following reason, it is likely to assume that a psychiatrist would spend days, even years, analyzing your words before making any drastic actions upon them, because we all know it takes a lot of time to understand the human mind.

Lewis: Yes.

Christian: Following reason, once again, is it not logical to assume that an imaginary dog would be able to know and accomplish what its creator wants?

Lewis: I don't understand?

Christian: For instance, Oscar would never be able to tell anyone that you wanted to burn your family to death. He would never be able to give them a warning signal, because he is an animal with a very small brain . . . Actually, an animal with no brain.

Lewis: Yes.

Christian: Following reason, one more time... If you told an arsonist, as we have already defined an arsonist, that you wanted to burn your family so that they would die, is it a likely assumption that the arsonist would burn your family?

Lewis: But Dan wouldn't have done that!

Christian: But he did! And not because he liked you, nor because he wanted to do you a favor. The arsonist, Dan, burned your family because he liked the orange, red, and yellow color of the flames. Those colors were all the incentive he needed to start the fire.

Lewis: I don't think that Dan would do . . .

Christian: That leaves us with two options. The first is that you were the arsonist, Lewis! You allowed your family to die a horrid death with no feeling of guilt. You allowed them to believe you were insane so you didn't have to admit what you had done! You created a psychiatrist and an imaginary dog to save yourself, to save your own life after you destroyed theirs!

Lewis: No! I wasn't . . .

Christian: You forget I know the truth. That's why I don't buy into that theory. Or at least not entirely.

Lewis: What do you believe then?

Christian: I do believe the truth, Lewis. And the truth is that you are Dan. You did it all and made up this alibi of insanity to get off the hook! You knew an imaginary pet and a fake psychiatrist could never tell anyone that Dan doesn't exist. They could never tell anyone that Dan doesn't exist. They could never tell anyone that you are Dan. But I know. And the rest of the voices know. Therefore, you will always know . . .

Lewis: Don't say that!

Christian: Live with the voices. They make your fate worse than death!

Lights are dimmed. The curtains are also closed in preparation for the next scene.

SCENE 6

Setting:

The scene begins with the stage covered in darkness. There are three spotlights. The first is focused on Lewis, the second on President Ford, and the third is focused on the statue of Abraham Lincoln. Lewis hears the voice of President Ford but cannot identify who it belongs to or where it is coming from. The only thing Lewis can identify is the statue of Abraham Lincoln.

Ford: Why do we allow people like you to exist?

Lewis: What . . .

Ford: Why do we allow people like you to exist?

Lewis: Who are you? And what . . .

Ford: Why are there people like you? The world would be better off if we didn't have people like you. The least we could do is lock all the people like you up! Or better yet, we could kill all of you! That would solve a lot of problems!

Lewis: What? Who are . . .

Ford: We should have killed you ages ago, Lewis! If only I had been in office . . .

Lewis: Abe . . .

Ford: We should kill the entire lot of you! It would save the government a lot of time and give it a lot more money to spend on important problems.

Lewis: Abe! Where are you? Why won't you help me today?

Ford: Abraham is dead! He can't save you today or any other day!

Lewis: But today . . . what day is today? When will it turn to tomorrow? Abe, I need answers! Where are you, Abe?

Ford: Abraham is gone!

Lewis: No! I see him! Abe! Abe! Why won't you listen to me? (*The spotlight on Abraham Lincoln is lit.*)

Ford: Shut up and listen, Lewis!

Lewis: Abe, I don't want to listen . . .

Ford: Ladies and gentlemen of the United States of America. We are gathered here today to rally a victory for the Democratic Party. We have made a major advancement in the election, and I hope to see it last for the next eight years.

With the end of this statement, the spotlights are taken off of the two men and the statue of Lincoln while the lights are raised. The audience is able to see a crowd of people standing and applauding as a new president stands behind the White House.

The new president is a short man. He is wearing a long, black coat that covers his black suit. His head is bare, covered by only a few remaining strands of hair that will surely leave him within the next four years. His voice is deep and powerful. Behind the crowd, Lewis can be seen sitting next to the statue of Abraham Lincoln.

Lewis: Is this going to be another speech, Abe? One of those speeches where nothing valuable is said, but everyone claps anyway? (*No answer.*) Why are you laughing, Abe? Are you laughing at the promises?

Ford: Throughout the past year, I have made many promises. I have issued claims that there will be changes which will benefit the American people. (*Crowd roars.*)

I am here today to talk about one of the most important issues of the twentieth century: capital punishment. It has been seen as an unjust and cruel punishment for individuals who have made mistakes in their lives. But with the increasing number of crimes in our country, we are left with only one option. "An eye for an eye and a tooth for a tooth," just as the Bible tells us! (*Crowd applauds.*)

Over the last century, we have seen an increase in the number of serial killers that exist in our society. Jeffrey Dahmer, Ed Gein, to mention a few. They have taken control of our society because they do not think that any court will sentence them to death. And you know what . . .

They are right! It has become easier to commit the heinous crimes that they do and receive a punishment of lifetime imprisonment. All because the people around them don't believe that killing them is a just solution. They cite mental problems and genes that these people possess that most ordinary people don't have. I want to tell you I don't care about any of that garbage! I believe we must make a statement against these people! We cannot allow them to run loose and damage the safety of our society for people like me and you.

Lewis: Abe, are you laughing anymore? Abe, why are you listening to him?

Ford: Crime has increased by fifteen percent in the last year. Criminals are commonly beginning to sneak through the judicial system with claims of mental insanity. I want to put an end to this! (*Crowd roars.*) I want to force criminals to accept the punishments they deserve for their actions! (*Crowd roars.*) I want the world to see we have as much control within our nation as we have throughout the world! (*Crowd roars.*) We can no longer show any signs of weakness! That is why I come before you today with a proposal. In my hand . . . (*President begins waving a scroll.*) In my hand, I hold a bill that I am going to present to Congress this working week. In the bill, I plan to force capital punishment on anyone proven guilty of murder. If someone kills another person, the government shall inflict the same punishment back on that person. I want the nation to be under control. I want our streets to be safe once again. (*Crowd roars.*)

This is the second step in the long process of gaining safety within our nation. As you know, the first was the passing of the Brady Bill, which forced criminals to wait seven days before they were allowed access to guns. It wasn't the law-abiding citizens that complained. It was the criminals! It has created some hassle for the common people, but at the same time, it has eliminated many problems. We made them wait so that they had clear heads when they committed their crimes.

Now, join me as we force the criminals in our society to make a definite choice! Help me make the majority of them choose between an action and a definite consequence for that action! When they make that choice, we will see if they accept the fact that they are opening themselves up for the punishment of death! (*Steam escapes the president's mouth as he finishes his speech, indicating a cool day. The crowd continues to roar as the president steps in front of the microphone once again.*) Why don't we kill all the lunatics! All the people like Lewis!

With this, the lights are dimmed and two spotlights are turned on, one on President Ford and the other on Lewis. The crowd exits the stage in darkness.

Ford: We should lock your kind away! You aren't crazy! You are just a murderer! The only difference between you and Ed Gein is that you started young! Though, I give you credit, you are cleverer than any other serial killer in this nation's history.

Lewis: I didn't murder anyone! I don't want to die!

Ford: Death is too good for you; that's why we are letting you live!

Lewis: Don't say that! I agreed with your speech . . .

Ford: Hello, Lewis. (*He speaks with a calm, sophisticated voice.*)

Lewis: How did you switch personalities like that? Is that what it means to control the voices?

Ford: I said, hello, Lewis.

Lewis: Hi.

Ford: How are you?

Lewis: What did you do with all the people? What did you do with Abe? Why did you not end your speech?

Ford: It doesn't matter. All that matters is, why did you do it?

Lewis: What did I do?

Ford: Lewis, I know your game better than you do. You can confuse Clare, Damon, and even Christian at times, because I know you don't always have to listen to your voice of reason unless you want to. But me . . . you can't confuse me. I know how your mind works because mine works the same way. I hear the voices, and I can change personalities at any moment. Do you want me to?

Lewis: No! I believe you. I just want to know what you want.

Ford: How did it happen, Lewis?

Lewis: Why should I tell you? You haven't told me anything about yourself! How do I know I can trust you?

Ford: Because I'm a politician.

Lewis: Politicians can't be trusted! That's a common fact in life! Nobody trusts a politician! Do you really expect me to talk to you and trust you?

Ford: I do.

Lewis: Why?

Ford: Because if you don't talk to me, I'll bring your dad back!

Lewis: You can't do that! Dad's dead! I killed . . .

Ford: Go ahead. Finish that sentence.

Lewis: I killed Dad. I killed Mom. I killed both my sisters. I killed my brother. I killed my dog. I killed everyone. I even killed those people at the church.

Ford: Why did you do it?

Lewis: You know why.

Ford: I know, but I want to hear you say it. I want you to tell me.

Lewis: What do you want me to tell you?

Ford: Lewis! Don't start! You can't fool me! I am just like you! Now, why did you do it?

Lewis: Because it felt like the right thing to do. I know it was wrong. I didn't want to do it, but I did it because . . .

Ford: Do you know the damage your actions caused the town?

Lewis: No.

Ford: You embarrassed them locally and nationally. People thought they were a town of lunatics. Whenever they hear the name of your town, they think of the pastor's kid who killed his family and lit the church on fire! They think of crazy people! How do you think it makes them feel to be a part of a town where everyone is considered insane because of one stupid, rotten kid?

Both spotlights are turned off. Only a few seconds later, another spotlight is turned on and focused on a man entering stage right. He has a black mustache and black hair. He appears to be in his early forties. His hair is parted on the left side, however, it is not combed. The man appears to have awoken from a nap, as if he was in a rush. He begins to speak to Lewis. Lewis can hear him, but he can't see him. The only thing Lewis can see is the statue of Abraham Lincoln.

Abe: It's nice when there isn't any light.

Lewis: What?

Abe: I was never much of a fan of the light. I always preferred darkness. The light always seemed to distract me from what I wanted to do.

Lewis: I like the light. I want to follow it when my life ends, but I'm not sure I know how.

Abe: What do you mean? You have talked of the light in the past and seemed to understand it. Why do you doubt your knowledge?

Lewis: I'm not sure . . .

Abe: Did someone teach you not to understand the light?

Lewis: No. No one has ever taught me about the light! Or, at least, taught me properly. I lived with a pastor for years, but he never showed me the light. He wasn't kind enough to show me the way.

Abe: You mean you lived in the darkness your entire life?

Lewis: Yes.

Abe: You've been alone.

Lewis: Yes.

Abe: You know the dark.

Lewis: Yes.

Abe: You want to see the light. (*No answer.*) Do you want to see the light, Lewis?

Lewis: Yes. The dark is so ugly.

The spotlights are turned off as Able flicks the light switch on the wall and moves to the table. The original room as found in Scene 1 is revealed to the audience. Lewis is sitting at the table while Abe is standing near the far wall.

The audience can easily see that Lewis still sees the statue of Abraham Lincoln. Lewis has changed little in appearance with the exception of graying hair.

Lewis: The dark is so ugly.

Abe: I disagree. I find the dark beautiful at times. It allows me to relax and examine my thoughts. It takes away the stress. That's why I wanted you to sit in the dark. I wanted you to examine your thoughts and relax.

Lewis: That's the problem. My thoughts add more stress than they relieve.

Abe: Yes, but if you control your thoughts, the darkness is a wonderful place.

Lewis: I understand. I found the darkness beautiful at first, myself. I even enjoyed it, but then . . .

A spotlight is shined on stage left while the rest of the lights are dimmed. The audience is able to see a memory that Lewis has.

He is four, and his father has taken him to a rally outside an abortion clinic. Lewis is able to see one particular girl who is being pummeled by rocks that people are throwing at her. People are yelling and screaming chants like, "Hit the bitch! Kill her, if she's going to kill the kid." But at the same time, these people are holding signs that say, "Stop the killing!" and, "Help save the life she doesn't want."

The audience can see Lewis in tears as a poor, defenseless Mom is being killed. Meanwhile, his father is standing, smiling at the girl's slow death. He is also smiling as he sees Lewis crying.

The spotlight is turned off as the lights are raised, and the focus of the stage is shifted back to Lewis and Abe.

Lewis: The darkness was beautiful, until I discovered that once you go in, you can never escape.

Abe: You can escape anytime you want to by turning on the lights.

Lewis: You don't understand.

Abe: What do you mean?

Lewis: The darkness grabs hold of you and possesses your soul. Then it possesses your mind. Once you enter, it is very difficult to step back, and then . . .

Abe: Then what?

Lewis: Then it controls you and doesn't allow you to leave. I didn't want to enter the dark, but someone talked me into it.

Abe: Who talked you into entering the darkness?

Lewis: That's not important!

Abe: What's important then?

Lewis: The important fact is that I entered the darkness. And, once I entered it, I became addicted.

Abe: What do you mean addicted?

Lewis: I had to have it all the time.

Abe: How so? I'm not sure I . . .

Lewis: First, it was my family. Then Oscar. Then Dan. Then the church. I couldn't resist. I tried to stop. I really tried to stop, but it was useless. The further I got into the darkness, the more I had to have it. It held so much control over me . . .

Abe: Who made you enter it?

Lewis: I'm not sure.

Abe: Was it your father?

Lewis: I don't know.

Abe: Was it your brother?

Lewis: I'm not sure.

Abe: Was it your therapist?

Lewis: I'm not sure.

Abe: Was it the politician?

Lewis: I'm not sure.

Abe: Was it Oscar?

Lewis: I'm not sure.

Abe: Was it Abraham?

Lewis: I'm not sure.

Abe: Was it your mother?

Lewis: I'm not sure.

Abe: Then who was it?

Lewis: I think it was all of them. They scared me. They all wanted me to do things that I didn't want to do. That's why I did everything opposite of what they said. I avoided them because I was afraid of what they had to say.

Abe: Are you still controlled and possessed by the darkness?

Lewis: I don't want to lose your support. I hate lying to you.

Abe: You won't lose my support!

Lewis: But . . .

Abe: Are you controlled and possessed by the voices?

Lewis: I'm not sure if I'm controlled by them or it.

Abe: An honest answer . . . How would you know if the darkness no longer controlled you? Or if the voices no longer possessed you?

Lewis: That's easy. If I didn't hear your voice and I was still able to see you, I would know I was all right.

Abe: When do you think you will find the light, Lewis?

Lewis: I'm not sure. I'm going to continue looking. I'll talk to you later.

Abe: Lewis! Don't go! . . . No! . . . Lewis! . . . Please don't go!

The lights are dimmed, and the curtains are closed.

SCENE 7

Setting:

When the lights are raised, Lewis Strange is seen sitting in the Arlington Cemetery. The sun is shining on what appears to be a beautiful spring day. The fields are all cut evenly and possess a beautiful green color.

Throughout the scene, a spotlight is focused on the statue of Abraham Lincoln, which can be seen in the background. The scene is very peaceful until Lewis and the audience hear the voice of Hillary. She is walking toward him, passing tombstone after tombstone.

Hillary: I want you to die! (*She shouts from a distance before coming closer and repeating.*) I want you to die!

Lewis: It can't be you . . .

Hillary: I want you to die!

Lewis: Yes! I know that! But I killed you first!

Hillary: I bore you! I brought your measly body into this world . . .

Lewis: And that's why I killed you, Mom! If you would've had your way, I never would have lived. Dad was the only one who wanted me brought into this world, and that was only because it would look bad for the pastor's wife to have an abortion.

Hillary: I never wanted an abortion!

Lewis: Yes, you did!

Hillary: How can you . . .

Lewis: Mom, I loved you when I was young, but then . . . then you started to listen to everyone else. You started to call me crazy for having all my friends that everyone said didn't exist. When I was little, you told me that I had a creative imagination. But, by the time I turned eight, you said I was too old to believe that I had imaginary friends . . .

Hillary: Lewis! Stop your whining and listen to me!

Lewis: But . . .

Hillary: Shut up! And listen to me . . . I loved you at first. Those stories I wanted you aborted from the beginning were false. I always loved you, but you . . .

Lewis: You never loved me!

Hillary: I loved you, but you scared me . . . You scared me when you tried to burn the living room down with Dan. So I overreacted and yelled, "I want you dead! I wish you were never born!" I didn't mean it, but it just kind of came out. I think it came out quicker because of all of the pressure I was getting from the rest of the town.

Lewis: But the doctor told me that Dan was a figment of my imagination. He doesn't exist, and he never did exist. I made that story up to right myself in the entire situation. To right myself for killing you and Dad and everyone else . . . Was he a figment of my imagination?

Hillary: Dan did exist. I didn't want to tell you this, but I suppose you need to know. Dan was the reason you turned dangerous. He was the reason I began to feel it was a mistake that I ever bore you. Dan was the one who got you playing with matches. Dan was the one who showed you what happened when gasoline and fire met. I tried to convince his parents, but they . . .

Lewis: What did his parents say?

Hillary: His parents said . . .

Lewis: What did his parents say?

Hillary: They said that you were the one who was crazy. You were the reason he started the fires. They said you would convince him to start fires. I didn't believe them, but it was hard to make other people believe me. Your father had seen you start the living room on fire twice. Everyone in the town knew you heard voices that didn't exist. They all knew you were different. Dan never seemed any different than the other kids until . . .

Lewis: Until what?

Hillary: Until he started to hang around with you, so naturally . . .

Lewis: Naturally, what?

Hillary: Naturally, they assumed that the fires were all your fault. They assumed that you were the reason that we died and the church burned down.

Lewis: But how did you know about that? You were dead, weren't you?

Hillary: Yes. I am dead . . . But up here, I hear about everything.

Lewis: Where's here?

Hillary: Never mind. I hate to see you blamed. I knew it wasn't you, but he had killed us so there was no one to defend you. There was no one to explain that you couldn't possibly have done what they said you did.

Lewis: How do you know?

Hillary: When were the fires committed?

Lewis: I don't understand . . .

Hillary: On what day did your house burn down?

Lewis: October thirteenth, nineteenth?

Hillary: You're close. I don't need the year. And on what date did the church burn down?

Lewis: The twentieth of the same month.

Hillary: Correct. And what did you do every Sunday?

Lewis: I can't remember.

Hillary: You went to church!

Lewis: No, I didn't! I never wanted to listen to Dad speak! I would never go to that place!

Hillary: Don't you remember when I found him beating you?

Lewis: No.

Hillary: He had you tied up in front of the fireplace. The rope was the tick brown kind that you usually found on boats. You were tied up in front of the fireplace, and he had a fire burning behind you. He was going irate. He was holding a whip, and I could tell by the marks on your chest that he had used it. (*Lewis feels his chest.*) He was holding a piece of iron in his other hand and appeared to be getting ready to brand you with it. I yelled at him and got him to stop. It wasn't easy, but I calmed him down so that he didn't hurt you anymore. When I finally made it to you, you were crying. I felt so awful. If I would have had a gun at that moment, I would have killed your father. But I didn't, so I did the next best thing that wouldn't hurt any of our reputations within the town.

Lewis: What did you do?

Hillary: Well, I couldn't tell the community about the events that occurred, because they would just say that the pastor was putting his crazy boy in line and that I was exaggerating the situation. So every Sunday, and as many other days as possible, I sent you to Reeseville to visit your grandma.

Lewis: Didn't the town question that?

Hillary: No. We would explain to them that we wanted you to have more than one perspective on the Bible. We also told them that it was the only time of the week that was convenient for you to visit your grandma.

Lewis: But didn't that make Dad angry?

Hillary: Yeah, but what could he do? If he said anything, he knew I could raise enough doubt about him within the town. And then he would be ruined.

Lewis: Wouldn't it benefit him? I mean, he would get rid of me.

Hillary: Exactly. If I made a ruckus and he won, he probably could have sent us both to a mental institution. Then he wouldn't have anyone to beat on, and he wouldn't have anybody to share . . . (*Her face turns red.*) Well . . . you know what I mean. Women aren't supposed to talk about things like that.

Lewis: You mean you allowed Dad to beat me so his reputation wasn't damaged in the community . . .

Hillary: It wasn't like . . .

Lewis: Let me finish! After you allowed Dad to beat me, you allowed him to make love to you! You allowed the community to think I was crazy when you were probably the one that knew I wasn't! You allowed Dan to hurt my reputation without talking to him! You allowed Grandma to believe . . . what did you tell Grandma?

Hillary: I told Grandma that I was unable to deal with you seven days a week. I told her that Dad wouldn't be able to afford it if you got up in front of the church and started to talk to your imaginary friends. I told her it wouldn't be good for his reputation, but I also told her I couldn't bear to see you put into a mental asylum.

Lewis: I'm glad I killed you!

The lights begin to fade as steam evaporates off the Memorial Pond in the background near Abraham Lincoln. Hillary exits stage right, and the lights eventually dim before the curtains close.

SCENE 8

Setting:

When the lights are raised, the audience is able to see a fort Lewis remembers from his childhood. The fort is built in a tree about ten yards into a forest. There is a door on the bottom and on the side. There are windows on the other two sides. The fort is painted orange and red. The audience can also see a bridge stretched from the fort to another tree about fifteen yards to the left. The bridge is made from the branches of an oak tree, making it very strong and stable. On the stem of the tree, the audience can see boards nailed to the tree about a foot apart all the way to the top. These are steps for people who are too weak to use the rope.

Before the forest, the audience can see a green pasture in which Lewis is playing. He is surrounded by green grass and the smell of fresh manure. A cow stands to his left.

Michele: London bridge is falling down . . .

Lewis: Who's there?

Michele: Falling down. Falling down. London Bridge is . . .

Lewis: Where are you?

Michele: Falling Down. Falling down. Falling down . . .

Lewis: I loved that park.

Michele: London Bridge is . . .

Lewis: I loved that fort.

Michele: Falling down. Falling down. Falling down.

Lewis: The butterflies and fireflies were always there. They would play with me.

Michele: London Bridge is . . .

Lewis: I remember playing war, diving in the mud, and feeling the comfortable scrape of the weeds against my face.

Michele: Falling down. Falling down. Falling down . . .

Lewis: We pretended we were soldiers fighting in a war in a foreign country. We hid in a fort . . .

Michele: London Bridge is . . .

Lewis: The fort was great. Nobody bothered me there.

Michele: London Bridge is . . .

Lewis: But why did I paint it in orange and red?

Michele: Falling down. Falling down. Falling down . . .

Lewis: And why did we build a second one in the tree across from it?

Michele: London Bridge is . . .

Lewis: Those steps . . . Dan built them, but . . .

Michele: Falling down. Falling down. Falling down . . .

Lewis: That singing is so annoying. Why won't she shut up? Why won't she finish the song?

Michele: London Bridge is . . .

Lewis: I should ignore her, but I can't. Why can't I ignore her?

Michele: Falling down. Falling down. Falling down . . .

Lewis: How come I had forgotten about that fort? And why did I paint it orange and red?

Michele: The London Bridge is . . .

Lewis: Three of us built it. There was Dan, myself, and . . .

Michele: Falling down. Falling down. Falling down . . .

Lewis: Dan started the fires, and I heard the voices, but what did . . .

Michele: Falling down. Falling down. Falling down . . .

Lewis: She was a cruel friend. She played with guns and shot soup cans. But the reason I really hated her was because she always made fun of me.

Michele: London Bridge is . . .

Lewis: I know who you are!

Michele: Falling down . . .

Lewis: I never liked your fuckin' song!

Michele: Falling down . . .

Lewis: Why do you always have to sing it?

Michele: Falling down . . .

Lewis: Why do you still sing it?

Michele: Lewis, you love me. You know why I sing it. The memory of your fort remains alive in the song. You know it. Come on, sing with me. London Bridge is falling down. Falling down. Falling down. London Bridge is . . .

Lewis: I don't understand. I never knew the words to that song. I hated that song. Why would I want to sing it?

The background lights are beginning to dim over Lewis's fort to give the audience the feeling that the fort is disappearing. Eventually the entire stage is dark. Two spotlights are turned on. One is focused on Lewis and the other on Michele.

Michele: The song tells you the history of your fort.

Lewis: Michele!

Michele: What?

Lewis: What happened to my fort?

Michele: Excuse me. Don't you mean *our* fort? The fort Dan, yourself, and myself built to hide from the rest of the world.

Lewis: Was that why we built it?

Michele: Don't you remember? All the other kids made fun of you because you were always talking to yourself.

Lewis: I remember.

Michele: All the girls made fun of Dan because he was ugly, and he would just stare at the matches whenever he could . . .

Lewis: What did they make fun of you about?

Michele: Doesn't matter . . .

Lewis: What did they make fun of you over?

Michele: I said, it doesn't matter!

Lewis: What did they make fun of you about?

Michele: That you were my brother, and that Dan was a close friend . . . But it doesn't matter . . . What matters is that I was the normal one. I knew your fort was going to be destroyed. I didn't want them to have the pleasure of destroying it. I loved you. So I didn't allow that to happen . . .

Lewis: What do you mean? Destroying it? The fort is still there, isn't it? I was there a week or two ago with Dan.

Michele: No, you weren't . . .

Lewis: The fort can't be destroyed. I'd go back if I only had a map. Why did I have to lose that map? If only I hadn't gone there a couple of weeks ago. Then I would have the map . . .

Michele: But you weren't there a week or two ago.

Lewis: What do you mean?

Michele: You couldn't have been there a week or two ago with Dan because . . . because Dan is dead.

Lewis: Dan's dead?

Michele: He died when somebody burned him.

Lewis: Dan got burned?

Michele: They found his body staked to a burning barrel down by the river.

Lewis: How could Dan die by fire? He loved fire. He knew all about it. Unless . . . unless I was the one that burned him. But I don't remember a river . . . What river?

Michele: The river that travels through town. You know this one. It has a creek and a small bridge that only pedestrians and bikers can pass over. You used to take me there in the fall. We would look at the colors on the trees. They changed colors all the time, especially in the fall. Remember, that's why you painted the fort orange and red.

Lewis: No . . . I don't . . . I painted it orange and red because . . .

Michele: The water was pretty to watch. It trickled past the rocks changing from blue to white all the time. It could never move the rocks, remember?

Lewis: I can't remember.

Michele: You and Dan went there a lot also. You called it the secret burning place because you guys lit fires near the bottom of it. You would watch the fires and tell stories.

Lewis: How did Dan die?

Michele: I told you that he was burned.

Lewis: Who burned him?

Michele: That's a dumb question! Who do you think burned him?

Lewis: Dan?

Michele: No. Dan never lit a fire in his life. That was a lie that Mom started so that people would believe that you weren't the cause behind those fires. Besides, do you really think that Dan would burn himself?

Lewis: Was I? . . .

Michele: No . . .

Lewis: Then who was . . . who was the person that tried to ruin my life and Dan's, too?

Michele: What do you mean tried? They did ruin your lives.

Lewis: Who is 'they'?

74

Michele: Mom and Dad.

Lewis: What?

Michele: Dad burned Dan down by the river. Mom burned the church.

Lewis: But I thought both of them were dead when all that happened? I thought they burned to death in the house when I escaped?

Michele: That's what they wanted people to believe. It was easier that way. They were able to get rid of you and the voices by faking their own deaths. They hated you, and they knew that the only way out was to make it look like your fault or Dan's fault.

Lewis: What did the town think about Dan's death?

Michele: They kept it quiet. You know, out of the papers. They simply said that a youth died by the river of unknown causes. The autopsy came up with no exact cause of death, even though there were many burns found all over Dan's body.

Lewis: Did he have burns on his body?

Michele: I saw them take his body away. He was broiled like a piece of hamburger meat. All of his skin had been burned and his bones were black. It appeared as though someone had tied him to a barrel, doused him and it with gasoline, and then lit it with a match. They must have watched him burn for pure pleasure.

Lewis: I don't understand. If Mom and Dad were responsible, were you and the others meant to go along with them, or did you really die?

Michele: I escaped. I was fortunate. I saw them one night after all the kids had gone to bed. They were setting out the gas cans. The rags that were used as torches were also being prepared. They hid them outside behind a bush and went to bed. The following day, Dad came home from work early. You were supposed to be there, but you hadn't come back yet. The rest of us were watching television.

Lewis: Where was I?

Michele: You were at the park with Dan. Anyway, I was curious. Something didn't seem right so I kept sneaking a peek in the kitchen. Mom and Dad were constantly arguing. She appeared to be having second thoughts or wanting to wait for some reason. Dad wanted to do it right away.

Lewis: Why didn't you say something?

Michele: It would have only prolonged the inevitable. After a few hours, they seemed to disappear. I left Sara and Christian watching television and walked back out. I was going to get rid of the gasoline. As I was walking out, I heard this nagging voice, but no one was there. I guess it was my conscious or subconscious trying to tell me something. So I paused for a moment . . .

Lewis: What happened?

Michele: Nothing. So I decided to head back for the house. But as I turned around, the house was suddenly covered in flames. It was almost as if the ground just burned upwards onto the side of the house. The fire raced systematically, attacking the walls, floors, and family members inside.

Lewis: Did you see me?

Michele: I saw you racing around the side of the house. I wanted to stop you, but I couldn't.

Lewis: Why couldn't you stop me?

Michele: At the same time I saw you, I also saw Mom and Dad running away. If I said anything, they would have known that I wasn't inside. And I didn't want to take that chance.

Lewis: But how did they plan on getting away with it if they knew I wasn't going to be inside when they lit the house on fire?

Michele: Apparently, they had been planning on saying that it was kids playing with matches, but you weren't there, so they couldn't say that. No one would believe them.

Lewis: So what happened to them?

Michele: Apparently, they fled. After I saw them leave, I tried to get your attention. But it was too late. You ran inside the burning house because you wanted to save Oscar. When they brought you out, you were in shock and never came out of it. I was left alone. I watched as the police tried to talk to you. You started to go insane. You were jumping personalities. It took the police a week and a half to get a real name from you. Everyone in the house was considered dead, but you.

Lewis: If I was in police custody, why did everyone think I started the other fires?

Michele: You were staying at Grandma's under a police guard. And no one could account for where you were at the time of the fires. As time went on and the police couldn't find any suspects, they simply said that you were the one that started the house on fire. They said that your insanity or shock or whatever it was, was just an act. I wanted to help you, but if I did, I had to worry about Mom and Dad finding me.

Lewis: Where did they go?

Michele: Apparently, they set up camp by the river. They lived off of canned food. Dan had seen the damage that the fire had taken on you. He was a good friend. He saw that he could have vengeance on your parents for framing you for the fire. One day he prepared himself to attack Mom and Dad. But then . . .

Lewis: Then what?

Michele: Then, one day, they caught him watching them cook some beans. They knew he could give away their secrets, so they were left with one option and . . . and they lit him on fire.

Lewis: Why did the police keep quiet?

Michele: Dad was the priest. It was easier to say that he had an insane child who burned the house down and everything in it, rather than saying that he was on the loose. It meant less paperwork and less work in general. They simply buried the evidence that proved otherwise.

Lewis: How do you know about this if it was supposed to be buried?

Michele: Simple. I uncovered all the paperwork.

Lewis: Don't you have to be a part of the police force to do that?

Michele: Yes.

Lewis: Then how can you . . .

Michele: What do you think I am, Lewis? Haven't you noticed my badge?

Lewis: But the name . . .

Michele: Emma Kenda.

Lewis: Who's Emma Kenda?

Michele: That's my name. I had to change it so that Mom and Dad would never know I survived. I liked them thinking I was dead. It gave me a chance to live without having to deal with Dad every day. That's why I went into the police force, so I could put bastards like Dad behind bars forever.

Lewis: So what happens now?

Michele: Well, you have to leave the darkness.

Lewis: I like it here.

Michele: If you leave the darkness, you will be able to meet me.

Lewis: I would like that.

Michele: I will save your name, and Mom and Dad will be looked for more intensely.

Lewis: Mom and Dad are being looked for?

Michele: As we speak. But I need you to come out of this state before I can do anything more. If you don't, I have no living eye witnesses.

Lewis: What about yourself?

Michele: I won't become a witness unless you become one.

Lewis: So I have to be sane again?

Michele: Yes.

Lewis: How long has it been?

Michele: A long time.

Lewis: How long is 'a long time'?

Michele: I'm not sure anymore. I stopped counting the years. Let's just say you aren't a young man anymore. Don't let them waste any more of your life. Help me catch them.

With these words, Michele fades off toward stage right. She has been edging closer and closer to that area during the end of her conversation with Lewis. Lewis is left staring at the statue of Abraham Lincoln, on which a spotlight has been lit. After a few moments, the spotlights are turned off and the curtains are closed.

SCENE 9

Setting:

Lewis Strange can be seen sitting on the steps of the Lincoln Memorial, staring at Abraham Lincoln. He appears to be obsessed with the eyes of the statue. A stranger approaches and invades the silence. The man has blond hair that occasionally falls into his eyes, blocking his vision.

Chuck: Is this seat taken?

Lewis: No . . . go ahead . . . but watch out!

Chuck: Watch out? . . . For what? . . . What should I watch out for?

Lewis: The snakes . . . They're all over this area.

Chuck: What snakes? Washington isn't known for having snakes. That's Africa and Australia, isn't it?

Lewis: Snakes aren't what they always appear.

Chuck: Washington isn't known for having snakes. I'm sure of it.

Lewis: Realistically, it isn't. But theoretically . . .

Chuck: Theoretically, what?

Lewis: Theoretically, there are more snakes in this city than in any part of the world.

Chuck: I'm not sure I follow . . .

Lewis: Look at these buildings. They are filled with snakes, and not one of them is like Abraham.

Chuck: Yes, but the snakes are well-liked. They're garden snakes that can't harm anyone.

Lewis: Don't tell the American people that! Those snakes can eat right through their heads! Look at what they've done to me and you!

Chuck: What? Everything that has happened to me has been my fault. No one else's. I'm the one that quit my job. I'm the one who turned my back on my family . . .

Lewis: Yes, but who forced you to make those decisions? Who imposed the laws and the regulations that eventually drove you here?

Chuck: I wasn't forced anywhere! I came here by myself . . . for . . .

Lewis: How long?

Chuck: What?

Lewis: How long you have been here, away from your family?

Chuck: Two years.

Lewis: What are you doing at a mental institution for two years if you aren't lacking a little substance upstairs?

Chuck: That's not the point. The point is . . .

Lewis: That's precisely the point. There is no other way to explain us.

Chuck: You're mentally ill. I just live at St. John's Mental Institute . . .

Lewis: The snakes imposed a ton of taxes and stole your job to put you here. Meanwhile, they stole my family and made me believe it was my fault. If they had their way, I might be convicted of killing JFK.

Chuck: You've got it all wrong . . .

Lewis: No, I don't! The entire world wants me here because they don't understand me.

Chuck: Don't you think that you are exaggerating just a bit?

Lewis: I may be, but the snakes up on that hill and in that grassy area over there have destroyed my life. They're not garden snakes. They are boa constrictors or vipers. You know, the evil ones that secrete poison and slowly suck off the blood that flows to your head until you eventually die!

Chuck: You aren't dead, are you?

Lewis: That's because they're still sucking my blood from me. They've been sucking for the past forty years, and I can feel the end coming.

Chuck: I'll take my chances . . . Now, is it all right if I sit down?

Lewis: Go head. Wait! Watch out for the headset I found!

Chuck: Where did you find it?

Lewis: Does it matter?

Chuck: You didn't steal it, did you?

Lewis: No. I don't steal. I'm better than that.

Chuck: How did you get it?

Lewis: I got it legally. I just don't want to tell you who gave it to me. Is that all right?

Chuck: I suppose, but what kind of music do you listen to?

Lewis: What?

Chuck: You heard me. What kind of music do you listen to?

Lewis: The Grateful Dead, Bob Marley, Suicidal Tendencies, The Rolling Stones, Bob Dylan . . .

Chuck: Do you like Guns n' Roses?

Lewis: I have a tape of them . . .

Chuck: No. I don't listen to them, if you want . . .

Lewis: What about . . .

Chuck: No. I don't listen to any music. Or at least, not anymore . . . What I'm trying to say is that I used to listen to all these groups, but then . . . they started to publicly support Charles Manson. (*The garment Chuck is wearing appears to become brighter in color.*)

Lewis: Ha! Ha! Ha! That's the funniest thing I've ever heard, stopping listening to a band because they support someone.

Chuck: That's not funny! I'm very serious about my beliefs!

Lewis: Where?

Chuck: You know what you were about to say. It doesn't matter where I come from. The important thing is that you don't show your stupidity and laugh at the important things like my beliefs . . . You're so young, and you have so much to learn.

Lewis: Why shouldn't I laugh at the important things?

Chuck: Don't you know who Charles Manson was?

Lewis: No . . . Why? Should I?

Chuck: It depends on what your intentions are and what they have been in the past.

Lewis: Was he the guy that killed someone?

Chuck: Sharon Tate.

Lewis: What about her?

Chuck: Charles Manson killed her, among others.

Lewis: So, he was a serial killer?

Chuck: A serial killer. He is the essence of the term 'serial killer'. He was the serial killer of the sixties. He makes Jack the Ripper look like a nice guy.

Lewis: That was before I was born. I don't want to remember the memories my parents told me of that period.

Chuck: That's the problem. No one wants to remember the awful parts of history because they are afraid of it repeating. But by forgetting, they allow it to repeat. You're the perfect example of that . . .

Lewis: What?

Chuck: I can't believe you've never heard of Charles Manson. You remind me so much of him.

Lewis: Who?

Chuck: What?

Lewis: Who do I remind you of?

Chuck: Charles Manson.

Lewis: One day, I want to run this country. I want to be the person in charge. I want to make all the decisions. I want to control everything and everyone!

Chuck: What?

Lewis: Nothing. Just mumbling nonsense to myself. Only a dream that can never happen.

Chuck: Anything can happen if you put your mind to it. After all, you are living in America, the land of opportunity. You can be sane or insane. You can have a family or be lone. It doesn't matter. It's your right to have whatever you want. All you have to do is choose . . .

Lewis: Did you say that Manson guy died?

Chuck: No. He's still living.

Lewis: What?

Chuck: They tried to electrocute him and failed. He was scorched with nasty burns, and his brains were fried, but they couldn't kill him.

Lewis: I can't believe they actually tried to kill him. That doesn't happen here. President Ford told me he would get that changed.

Chuck: It happens here, but only for the special ones.

Lewis: Why didn't they kill Manson after that?

Chuck: Because the voters went crazy. Capital punishment is cruel. Capital punishment shouldn't be allowed. Eventually, there were so many people against killing him that he wasn't allowed to be killed.

Lewis: Don't they know that's what we all want? The chance to die quickly and end our lives. End all the gruesome voices.

Chuck: What? Did you say you hear voices?

Lewis: Yes.

Chuck: Why do you hear the voices?

Lewis: What?

Chuck: Why do you hear the voices?

Lewis: What?

Chuck: Why do you hear the voices?

Lewis: I'm not sure . . . I never really . . .

Chuck: Do you think hearing the voices makes you insane?

Lewis: No. But I wish they did. Then the voices would be easier to handle. I wouldn't have to fight them as much. I could simply do and believe what they tell me.

Chuck: What voices do you hear?

Lewis: People from my past.

Chuck: Where do they talk to you from?

Lewis: What do you mean?

Chuck: Where do they come from?

Lewis: My past.

Chuck: How can the voices that come from your past talk to you?

Lewis: I don't know. They just do. And then a new one joins the old ones every year. After a while they fade away. But by then, there are so many that I'll never be left alone. I'll never get a moment's peace.

Chuck: I still don't understand. Where do they come from?

Lewis: I'll tell you what the doctors told me. Someday, one of them will tell me where they come from, how they formulate, and why they do this to me.

Chuck: Who?

Lewis: What?

Chuck: Who will tell you?

Lewis: Who do you think?

Chuck: The doctors.

Lewis: Possibly.

Chuck: The snakes.

Lewis: Maybe.

Chuck: The voices.

Lewis: Aren't they the same?

Chuck: Where do they come from?

Lewis: I don't know. I thought you would be able to tell me. Abe said you had them. Abe said everyone had them, except that other people knew where to hide them.

Chuck: Where?

Lewis: Where what?

Chuck: Where do other people hide them?

Lewis: I don't know.

Chuck: The subconscious . . .

Lewis: What?

Chuck: The subconscious. It's part of your mind.

Lewis: How do you know if something's a part of my mind? You haven't been inside here! (*Lewis points to his head.*) How would you know if I have one?

Chuck: Everyone has one. It's a simple fact of nature.

Lewis: Did you ever think that I might not have one? That could explain me.

Chuck: What needs to be explained? I understand you.

Lewis: That's impossible.

Chuck: President Ford understood you.

Lewis: No, that can't be. The only who understands me is Abe.

Chuck: Abe . . . You've mentioned Abe many times in our conversation.

Lewis: Yeah . . .

Chuck: Who is he?

Lewis: He . . . I'm not sure . . .

Chuck: Is he a voice?

Lewis: No, but I've told you way too much.

The stage lights fade to black.

SCENE 10

Setting:

Lewis Strange is seen sitting in the original room once again. Abe is seen sitting across from him. He is cleaning up a Coke can and a hamburger wrapper. Mustard and ketchup are smeared across the table.

Behind Abe, Rita can be seen. Behind her, sunlight can be seen sneaking into the room through the open window.

In this scene, the room is positioned on stage right, leaving room on the other side of the stage for simultaneous action.

Abe: This trash is everywhere! Why hasn't someone cleaned it up? I want an answer! . . . I'm sorry, Lewis, I told someone to clean up when you finished eating.

Rita: I'm sorry, I was supposed . . .

Abe: Don't let it happen again! Someone should always be cleaning up the trash!

Lewis: I had someone say that about me yesterday . . .

The lights on stage left are raised. Two men can be seen walking near the Washington Monument. One man, Owen, appears to be in his early forties. His eyes are blue, and his hair is graying. He is staring at Lewis, who is sitting on the steps of the Washington Monument in a bum-like fashion.

The second man, Allistar, is dressed in a brown Armani suit. His clothing is mostly brown.

As the audience watches the action on stage left, Lewis Strange can be seen on stage right, explaining the action on stage left to Abe. As in previous scenes, a second actor will be needed to play Lewis Strange. The audience cannot hear this conversation between Abe and Lewis, because the lighting is such that the audience's attention is focused on stage left.

Owen: Look at this vagrant! I can't even walk to work in the morning anymore without having to look at these worthless bums. Why don't they clean up or something? Or at least find a way to keep them from finding the lawns and steps in front of our sacred monuments.

Allistar: I agree, Owen. It's been too long that we have been lenient on these people. Maybe we should start blocking off land in a city or in the country and put all of them there. Block it off and never let anyone out.

Owen: You're describing a concentration camp.

Allistar: I guess you could call it that . . .

Owen: I'm not sure I agree with you. I mean, don't you think that's taking it a bit far?

Allistar: It might be . . . I mean, it was only a suggestion.

Owen: All I'm trying to say is that I'm getting sick of people like this always begging and performing, expecting money from people like me. I just want to walk to work without feeling guilty. But that can't happen until all these people disappear.

Allistar: Come on. Let's get out of here. If we stay any longer, we might get robbed by the trash on the steps.

The lights fade on stage left and, therefore, the audience's attention is focused back on Lewis and Abe. Through the mirror behind the table, the audience can now see Michele and Damon observing Abe and Lewis's conversation.

Abe: When did this happen, Lewis?

Lewis: I can't remember.

Abe: How did it make you feel?

Lewis: It made me feel like I was trash.

Abe: But you aren't trash!

Lewis: How do you know?

Abe: Because you're human.

Lewis: No, I'm not!

Abe: You are! You have a soul and a mind! You just haven't directed it in the right way yet! Someday you will.

Lewis: But I can't remember what I do! I'm abnormal because I can't find the light!

Abe: Lewis, will you let me help you?

Lewis: I'm not sure . . .

Abe: Will you let me lead you out of the darkness?

Lewis: Where will I go when you lead me out?

Abe: You know as well as I that you can't go back to the light. Therefore, I will lead you beyond the light to a great place.

Lewis: I don't want to go there!

Abe: I can bring you reality.

Lewis: I don't want reality!

Rita: But reality wants you!

Lewis: What?

Rita: Reality wants you!

Lewis: Who said that?

Rita: Turn around, Lewis.

Lewis: Why?

Rita: Because reality wants you.

Lewis: Who are you?

Rita: I am reality, and I have come to claim you since you won't allow Abe to do it.

Lewis: I hate reality! It only tries to hurt me!

Rita: No, it doesn't. Reality is trying to save you.

Lewis: Save me from what?

Rita: Yourself.

Lewis: I don't need to be saved. I'm perfectly all right by myself. All I need is for these voices to leave me alone.

At this point in the play, Lewis Strange begins to beat his head on the table. After a few moments, blood begins to form on Lewis's forehead. Lewis Strange stops pounding his head as soon as Rita begins speaking, but no sooner. The entire time Lewis is beating his head, a muffled cry can be heard from Lewis as he screams, "I'm going to beat these voices out!"

Rita: But that is the purpose of reality. It will destroy the voices.

Lewis: No, it won't!

Rita: What will reality do then?

Lewis: Reality will destroy me! Reality created the voices! Reality destroyed the bodies that belonged to the voices! Reality has left those voices with me!

Rita: No, it was your imagination that left you with the voices. We want to take them away. Follow me, Lewis.

Lewis: I'm not sure . . .

Rita: Just give me a chance. Will you give me a chance?

Lewis: I suppose.

Rita: Abe is your friend?

Lewis: Yes.

Rita: Abraham is a part of reality?

Lewis: Yes.

Rita: Then reality owns one friend?

Lewis: Yes.

Rita: The therapist across from you is your friend?

Lewis: Yes.

Rita: He is also from reality?

Lewis: Yes.

Rita: Therefore, reality owns two friends.

Lewis: Yes.

Rita: How many does imagination allow?

With this question, the lights on stage right are lit, and a little girl is standing next to a swing set. The attention is taken away from Rita and given to Sara. She is a four-year-old girl with blue eyes. Her voice is hard to understand as she attempts to fight her urge to sob. Tears can be seen forming in her eyes and slowly dripping to her cheeks and the ground beneath her feet. Her golden hair is positioned in a ponytail.

Sara: Do you want to play?

Lewis: Not now, I'm busy.

Sara: Please play with me.

Lewis: Shut up! I'm talking to someone!

The lights on stage right are turned down, and the audience sees Abe grab Lewis's wrist. Abe stares into Lewis's eyes.

Abe: So that's the problem? If you leave the world of the voices, you will lose your sister forever. You already lost her once, and you don't want to lose her again.

Lewis: No, it isn't!

Abe: Lewis . . .

Lewis: Why are you always attempting to be a psychiatrist?

Abe: Because I am.

Lewis: You are not Abraham.

Abe: You're right. I don't sit on a throne in Washington D.C. I sit in a chair in a room at St. John's Asylum for the mentally challenged, with you. We sit together in Seattle. Although that normally allows me to escape to Washington . . .

Lewis: I wish I could escape . . . escape this world with all these . . .

Abe: With what? . . . With the voices?

Lewis: I want to escape.

Abe: You can. It isn't that difficult. All you have to do is listen to Rita and myself. Then you will come back to reality. You will kill the voices and the pain they cause you.

At this point in the scene, the lights are dimmed, and the spotlights are focused on the characters that speak for the rest of the play. The characters will enter as they did in Scene 1. This means that they will leave stage left if they enter stage left. It also means that if a character enters stage right, the next is to enter stage left.

Dan: Burn them! Burn them all! Come on! Burn them, and we can go play in the park!

Lewis: I don't want to burn them! They make sense. They speak logically. They are my friends!

Dan: No! I am your friend! I am your only friend! Don't you remember all those days we spent together in the park! There was no one else! It was me and you!

Lewis: But . . .

Dan: But nothing! Don't you remember how we started everything on fire and destroyed what we didn't like?

Lewis: But, I never . . .

Dan: Shut up! Don't you remember the explosions? They were so neat and powerful! You always like a good explosion!

Lewis: I don't want to burn things anymore!

Christian: You don't really want to lose the explosions, do you?

Lewis: No.

Sara: Lewis, play with me.

Rita: Reality will not go away. You will always be able to find us, but soon we will not stay around so you can talk to us anytime you want. Abe and I will leave.

Michele: Did he talk yet?

Lewis: Who's that?

Abe: It's Michele. She wants you back, too. She loves you. She's part of your family, and she misses you.

Lewis: Yeah, but she's not Sara. She never loved me or Sara. She just wants to see Mom and Dad in jail.

Michele: Lewis! That's not true! I have always loved you. I will always love you. You are my brother. Come on! Listen to them! Come back to reality!

Christian: Is it logical to go back, Lewis? What has reality given you? Nothing! What would you do for a job when you went back?

Where would your money come from? Here, you can live and tease them. In return they feed you and make sure you talk to us. Who will be your audience if you go back to reality?

Lewis: I can live with my sister. I won't need you! I won't need an audience!

Michele: Yes! You can live with me!

Rita: Yes! You can live with her!

Sara: Does this mean we aren't going to play anymore?

Christian: What about her, Lewis? Where does she fit into reality? . . . I'll tell you . . . She doesn't! She is dead in reality!

Jilie: Lewis will go back. He likes to kill people! He is just a killer! He has been since the day he was born! He just doesn't want to admit it!

Lewis: Shut up, Jilie! I'm not a killer; I have never killed before! I know I'm right, because they told me so!

Jilie: Who told you so?

Lewis: The people from reality told me! I know I am right, because you died in the fire! I never liked the way you cleaned our house anyway!

Bill: Then how do you explain . . .

Hillary: What happened to us?

Bill: Your beloved father . . .

Hillary: And mother.

Bill: We are here . . .

Hillary: Even though you killed us.

Bill: How do you know you can believe your sister?

Hillary: How do you know she didn't do what she says we did?

Bill: How do you know?

Rita: What's happening?

Abe: Talk to us, Lewis.

Lewis: Mom and Dad want me to explain that Michele didn't do what she says they did.

Michele: I can help on this one.

Through the darkness toward the stage right, a door is opened. A guard escorts an old couple through the door. Both individuals have gray hair and appear to be on their deathbeds. The man needs a cane to walk, while the woman needs a stroller.

Michele: Here are Mom and Dad. They have been brought in for questioning. I just couldn't wait for you anymore. I didn't want them to get away with what they did to me and you.

Bill: I'm not sorry!

Hillary: We didn't do anything!

Bill: It was that vagrant!

Hillary: We aren't his parents!

Bill: You can't prove we are!

Michele: But I can! Lewis, I traced their records. I have a match. This is Mom and Dad. I got them! Now, let's make them pay!

Rita: Make them pay, Lewis!

Lewis: Let's make them pay!

Clare: What about Damon and myself? After all we've done for you, you're going to kill us and go to those other doctors?

Lewis: What about my doctors? Can they come, too?

Rita: We're here.

Lewis: No! I mean Clare and Damon.

Rita escorts a bailiff close to Lewis and points to a name tag.

Rita: Lewis, read that for me.

Lewis: It says Damon.

Rita: That's right. You spent so much time with him that you made into part of your mind. Especially after that one time you attacked him. In order to save himself, he had to beat you up pretty bad.

Damon: Sorry about that.

Lewis: What about Clare?

Abe: We don't know where you got her from.

Rita: Hopefully, someday you will be able to tell us.

Sara: Don't leave me. Everyone is leaving so fast. I just want to play. Play with me before you go to the park.

Dan: You can't play with her! You have to play with me and start things on fire!

Jilie: You can't play with him, unless you want to burn in hell forever!

Bill: Yes, he got you to burn me!

Hillary: And me!

Clare: Do you really have to face reality?

Ford: We should have killed you a long time ago! All insane people are worthless!

Allistar: That's because they are nothing. You're nothing! Aren't you, Lewis?

Rita: You're sane. Tell me your name.

Lewis: My name is Lewis Strange.

Damon: She's right. You are sane.

Christian: Is it logical that you're sane? After all, you wouldn't still hear us if you were sane, would you?

Abe: Lewis, are you there? We can't afford to lose you. Otherwise, they might lock you up forever.

Michele: I want these two put in jail!

Abe: What is your name?

Lewis: My name is Lewis Strange.

Chuck: No, it isn't!

Lewis: Shut up!

The lights go off, and the curtains close.

.

www.ingramcontent.com/pod-product-compliance
Lightning Source LLC
Chambersburg PA
CBHW071319090426
42738CB00012B/2731